Country Style

Living the Farm Life

By Doris Stensland

_____

Cover Drawing and Illustrations by Doris Stensland

Country Style – Living the Farm Life

Copyright © 2004 by
Doris Stensland

Library of Congress
Control Number: 2004096832

ISBN 0-9759456-1-0

Stensland Books
3121 South 102 Street
Omaha, Nebraska 68124
www.stenslandbooks.com

Printed in United States of America
By
Husker Midwest Printing
Omaha, Nebraska

Preface

This book is a collection of *Country Style* columns which were written for a County weekly newspaper in the late 1960's. It light- heartedly records the daily events of farm life then. It shows how the farm animals entertained us with their antics and burdened us with concern for their welfare. These animals added a warm feeling to farm life, and put the heart in farming.

Now farming has changed. During the last fifty years, there has been an exodus of the milk cows, pigs and chickens from the majority of farmsteads. This has left today's farms with only complicated giant machinery.

May this book recall for you the days of milk cows, pigs, chickens and lambs, and leave you once again with the warm feeling of those days.

I want to thank the *Sioux Valley News* of Canton, South Dakota for granting permission to reprint these columns, and I want to credit my daughter, Susan, for the idea of putting this book together, and for persistently laboring to get it accomplished.

Country Style

November 24, 1966

Welcome to the Country! It isn't a fancy place. That's why we like it. It's a place where life doesn't speed by so frantically. Where things are matter-of-fact. It is an interesting place where common everyday things happen. Like a newborn calf trying out its legs and learning to drink from a pail. Simple things. Complicated things.

Farming is a strange mixture of miracles and sweat-of-the-brow; where the sun and the rain and God's blessings are necessary. I hope the flavor of the country will tease you and maybe get you to love it.

Corn-picking season is almost over. It is a rewarding time, and a dangerous time. As the corn pickers are parked for another year, the wives and mothers breathe easier again.

Corn-picking time has its special noises. When the tractor motor roars into a noisier gear and I hear the banging of the steel elevator I know another wagon of corn is being unloaded. I like to watch the golden ears being carried up the elevator and catapulted into the crib. The clickity-clack of the elevator reminds me of the store's cash register as the receipts are placed in the till. Albeit, the farmer's version is larger and noisier.

I'm glad I don't raise chickens. Partly because of the work that goes with it, but mostly because this gives me an excuse to go down the road and buy eggs from my neighbor. Usually this includes a cup of coffee and a visit. Those of you who buy eggs in the store may get green stamps with your eggs, but I am given the bonus of having my spirits lifted, and my neighbor has a special way of knowing how to give encouragement.

It seems like Thanksgiving has to give us a nudge before we stop to count our blessings. It reminds me of when the children were small and I was trying to teach them to say "Thank you." How often I had to prompt them with the familiar, "now what do you say?" Why is it so hard to get the "thank-you's" out?

Have you counted your blessings lately? Er..."now what do you say?"

Country Style

December 1, 1966

Now that things have slipped down into a slower gear my husband has time to come into the house for his morning coffee. At the kitchen table we can leisurely talk and catch up on each other's dreams and plans. The practical ones and the daydream ones.

Usually I hear a wistful remark about a certain new piece of green machinery. But when I hear the price I do believe it must be made of gold!

Each morning the cattle patiently wait at the gate to be turned into the freshly harvested corn field. It sort of reminds me of people on bargain day. As the gate opens, they rush out to find a tasty bargain before someone else discovers it.

Fall has an uncluttered beauty all its own. The changing picture from my kitchen window always gives me something to enjoy. The colors on nature's palette have changed from rich colors of autumn to plainer ones. Strips of black plowing make designs in the countryside. The golden piles of corn glimmer in the sunshine and the bare trees stand in dark brown. But the sight of the black and white Holsteins, prim and stately, alongside the bright red barn and the black calves trying to poke their heads between the wooden rails of the fence delight both my eyes and my heart.

If anyone heard me call our dog, he would surely wonder. When I realize what I'm asking as I call, "Here, Troubles", I am relieved to see only the dog come in response to my call.

Have you ever watched a farmer as he picks up one of his biggest, most perfect ears of corn? He looks at it with pride and satisfaction. Now he feels the months of toil have been worthwhile. These golden ears are his paycheck. And deep down inside he really knows that he is just a "partner".

It was God that changed the little kernel he planted this spring into the green blade of summer and now the golden ears of harvest. And he is thankful that the partner he works with is better at multiplying than adding and subtracting!

Country Style

December 8, 1966

Everyone is getting ready for the onset of winter. Even the pony has taken on a warmer, shaggier coat. And the farmer is busy these days getting all the loose ends tied up so chores won't be too difficult when winter comes in earnest. He has many mouths to feed, come snow or shine.

Along the countryside you can see silos jutting up here and there, stretching above the treetops. The housewife preserves her fruits and vegetables in quart jars, but the farmer preserves his feed in these tall, giant-sized containers.

If you have never seen nor smelled silage, I would describe it as sort of a cole slaw - with a plus. It is the specialty of the feed yard.

But on washday it's a nuisance. Those little bits drizzle out of every pocket and cuff. It takes lots of shaking and emptying before the coveralls are fit for the machine.

Our country school program is coming up in a few days. It holds almost as much excitement as Christmas itself. I believe a country school teacher must be part magician to be able to come up with such delightful programs with her limited cast.

Late every afternoon I can look out my kitchen window and watch the homecoming parade. The long procession of cows is headed by a leader, who sets the pace. The rest follow in single file - not to the brisk step of a marching band, but with a leisurely, contented gait. I can just imagine banners waving over them saying "Drink More Milk".

I saw my husband silhouetted against the sky as he was getting down silage from his brim-full silo. He looked so small way up there that I couldn't' help but ask, "What is man that Thou art mindful of him?" And then I thanked Him because He was.   Ps. 8:4

Country Style

December 15, 1966

The "oohs" and "aahs" you hear at a stuffed toy counter can't compare with the reactions to our real live puppies. They are just old enough to waddle around, and they'll steal your heart. On these cool days you'll find them all cuddled together in a puppy pile. With two dogs and a batch of puppies, we have to milk one cow just to satisfy the dogs and cats.

ON CHRISTMAS baking days my kitchen is filled with pleasant baking fragrances inter-mingled with pleasant memories of two dear aunts and a grandmother. Every year I use their recipes and recall other Christmases when we feasted on their Christmas delicacies. But my efforts never quite measure up to their culinary success.

It's a good thing God gives us winters. I'm sure if our growing season was year-round the farmers wouldn't be satisfied with only one harvest. They need winter to force them into a slower pace.

AT THIS time of the year I really appreciate our mail box, and would like to say "thank you" to the person who thought up rural free delivery. These days our mail box almost seems to beam with its load of happy Christmas mail.

What would Christmas be like without cards and letters? The five-cent stamp provides a visit with loved ones that time and distance wouldn't permit. These cards and letters are the cement that helps hold friendships and family together.

But there have been other days when our mailbox must have been almost ashamed to unload its contents of bills and advertising.

EVERYWHERE we go there are decorations, music and the Christmas rush. But on the farm it feels good to get out under the evening sky and enjoy some real quietness.

Here are no loud-speakers or blaring music, and the only Christmas hangings are the stars above. Then I am reminded of the first Christmas when it was so still they could hear the angels sing.

Country Style

December 22, 1966

'Twas the night before Christmas and down on our farm
The barnyard lay basking in its usual calm.
But Christmas made everything different tonight.
It invaded my thoughts and brought me delight.
Now all my wandering eye could perceive
Reminded me of the first Christmas Eve.

The manger was here with the sweet-smelling hay.
(I envisioned the Babe who that night in there lay.)

A cow, chewing her cud, turned 'round to stare
When she discovered me standing there.
She looked so wise.
I could but surmise she was trying to say,

**"My ancestor was there that first Christmas day.
She gave up her stall as a gift for the King.
Now, may I ask, have you given anything?"**

No donkey have we - but our pony's the size
Of the one that bore Mary Bethlehem-wise.

Our one pet sheep nudged and whispered to me

**"My forefathers were there on the hills to see
The angel hosts sing and make the sky bright.
Have you heard their message and worshiped tonight?"**

The dogs keep watch the long night through
And the kittens purr, "I'm glad to see you."

Yes, the barnyard is always a friendly place
And it must have been so in the Christ-child's days.
'Twas here God delivered His son to this earth
And the friendly animals greeted His birth.

May the joys of Christmas delight your eyes, ears and palate - But most of all, your heart.

Country Style

December 29, 1966

Most of us are still enjoying Christmas and special visits with loved ones. The hearts of both young and old are busy clicking snapshots of little and big joys and developing them into precious memories to be treasured and enjoyed for a lifetime.

BOTH morning and evening chores must now be done by artificial light. The sun is a regular sleepyhead these days. He retires while it is still afternoon, and of late he has been very reluctant to get up in the morning to rise and shine.

But the REA saves the day. How hard it would be to milk by lantern-light. And dangerous too. That's how Mrs. O'Leary's troubles started.

THERE HAS been a battle going on in our barn these last few days. These skirmishes are known as "the taming of the heifer." The spunk of a young cow can try the patience of the most patient farmer. In the process of getting a heifer accustomed to being tied and hobbled the farmer has to be prepared for assaults from all four quarters. So far, the bucket is all she has been able to kick around.

I understand the schedule calls for more of these opponents coming up.

THE FARMER is busy with his end-of-the-year bookkeeping. About this time he finds out there are bigger things than income - for instance, bills! And the job that takes the joy out of this holiday time is getting them settled up.

His bookkeeping shows him whether it would be wiser to make a sale before January 1st or wait until after.

ON THE threshold of a new year we always have mixed feelings. We would like to stand on tiptoe and peek inside, and at the same time we feel like a little boy afraid to go into a dark room - a bit apprehensive of the unknown.

But the little boy will enter in confidently and expectantly when he has his little hand safely inside his father's strong one...and so can we!

Country Style

January 5, 1967

We have a new big commission firm calendar on the wall again. The only honest compliment I can give it is that the dates are in big bold print.

Each year I dream of receiving a colorful calendar with a pretty scene for each month of the year, yet with numbers big enough to be seen from our places at the kitchen table. But this black and white one does serve the purpose.

OUR TROUBLES is gone. We gave away her puppies and it broke her mother-heart. I suppose she is still frantically searching the countryside for them.

Animals certainly take their mother-responsibility seriously. Ever so often a cow will carry on. She will stand outside the barn for days and moo for her calf until she is hoarse. Her little calf is safe inside in a warm pen, but she feels personally responsible for it.

God in His wisdom placed this maternal instinct inside animals or else whatever would happen to all the helpless newborn creatures in the world?

IN GETTING ready for winter some farmers have made a few changes in the landscape. Nice large, loaf-shaped haystacks that were standing in the hayfield a few weeks ago now rest in the farmyard. But it didn't happen by magic. If you had been around you would have seen the hay-mover transport a whole haystack intact. Just like house-moving.

To the cow, hay is the staff of life. It can be compared to bread in our diet.

When the food is close to the animals the farmer need not worry about bad weather cutting off his supply. It's just like keeping a few extra loaves of bread on reserve in the freezer in case of a blizzard.

ANOTHER year is past and we have made our mark on it. Ahead are new days to live, to love and to labor in. 365 days when "His mercies will be new every morning". What can be better than that? Lam. 3:23

Country Style

January 12, 1967

About this time of the year our green acres turn to white and we get to make use of scoop shovels and 5-buckle overshoes, and the muscles that go with shoveling.

During snow weather the cows and pony become all bewhiskered with this white stuff. Often icicles hang from their faces and give them a grotesque look.

NOW MY kitchen window frames a Christmas card scene. I can look out upon the peacefulness of a farm winter landscape.

A covering of white makes the barn redder, and is a contrast to the black and white cows and the accents of green machinery.

The snow covers the drab and lifeless earth with its furry heaven-sent mantle. But how quickly the soil of this old earth dirties its pure whiteness.

The farmer's eye isn't trained to notice its beauty. He is liable to consider the extra work that goes with snow: feed bunks and feed floors to be shoveled, and the extra effort it takes to trudge the many paths he must travel in his daily chores.

THE LUMBER yard delivered another feed bunk the other day. With the new heifers enlarging the herd there just wasn't enough eating room around the feed bunk table. So my husband did what I do when I get a few more mouths to feed - add another leaf to the table!

DID YOU see the "Give Yourself a Lift" projects in a January farm magazine? It suggests that husbands and wives spend January in a February 14th mood. "Have a special date each week. Plan things to do together and don't spare the romance."

These will be moments to be remembered when life becomes a busy grind in midsummer.

OUR 4-H'ER raised a pet lamb for her project last year. It has outgrown its lambhood, but it is still a pet. There is still a strong attachment between sheep and mistress.

From the first thing in the morning until the last thing at night our 4-H'er has the welfare of her sheep on her mind. At breakfast she asks, "Dad, how's my sheep today?" After school she personally checks up on it and before going to bed we hear, "Is my sheep safe in the barn?"

She has a real shepherd's heart.

And I am given a good picture of the 24-hour-a-day concern the Good Shepherd has for me! Ps. 23

Country Style

January 19, 1967

It's funny, but the cows and pigs always manage to break out when I'm home alone. It happened again the other day. Pepper's persistent barking aroused my curiosity. From the window I saw a cow enjoying her new-found freedom by investigating things on our side of the fence.

I grabbed my jacket and ran out for I had visions of our whole herd of cows soon on the highway. There I discovered someone had neglected to fasten the gate.

That day a dog was a woman's best friend, for Pepper had chased the cow back in and was laying in the opening while a semi-circle of cows stared at her.

This is the first time Pepper has shown us her talents and I'll have to agree she's worth her gravy-train.

NOW THAT the trees are bare we can see all the bird nests. There is something sad about empty bird nests. They remind us of the happier days when they held little birds and the grove was full of twitter and song.

It makes us think of our own little nests. But really, if the nests here are empty, it only means that some place else the birds that flew away are busy building new little nests. And thus time marches on.

HAVE YOU ever noticed all the different shapes and sizes of corn cribs? There are mountain-shaped piles, neat cribs with tin roofs, little muffin-shaped ones and two and three tiered ones.

Some are tightly corsetted and held firm with red wooden stays. Some are so tightly fastened you can almost hear them groan in their discomfort.

And then there are those patterned after the architecture of the leaning tower of Pisa.

In some yards there is a conglomeration of all sizes and shapes. Temporary cribs and permanent cribs. Corn cribs full of corn and running over.

And I am reminded of the farmer in Luke 12:16 who got too busy building corn cribs.

Country Style

January 26, 1967

It's income tax time and the farmer is digging out his 12-month collection of papers, receipts, checks, etc.

These days he sits in the midst of this paper array and adds and subtracts columns of figures. But what he is really trying to do is solve this mystery - "Where did the money go?"

HOUSEWIVES are enjoying the fruit of their labors as they bring up jar after jar of tasty things from the basement. The chore they had preparing them is now overshadowed by the eating pleasure it gives the family.

We are sampling the apple butter I struggled with last fall. I haven't forgotten how I stirred and stirred this boiling mixture as it "plopped" and spurted me with little hot pellets.

But it certainly tastes good now!

DURING THE years that a child takes piano lessons a mother listens to a variety of exercises, scales, wrong notes and beautifully memorized pieces.

Now my listening brings me June in January as ten fingers practice MacDowell's "To a Wild Rose".

This plaintive melody brings to mind the fragrant upturned face of this humble little rose that grows neglected in hayfields, roadsides and uncultivated places. The farmer is well acquainted with it.

OUR CALF "nursery" at feeding time is an interesting place. These little ones require a lot of personal attention.

Teaching a newborn calf to drink from a pail can be a messy job. In its enthusiasm, the calf will lunge at the pail and the farmer must keep a firm grip on things. By the time he is through with lesson Number 1, the farmer's hand has been soaked in milk and his coveralls thoroughly splashed. Fortunately, the calves catch on by the second or third feeding.

Then the ones that have mastered this art must have their milk. Feeding five or six hungry mouths at once has its problems. The calves' impatience makes it difficult to end up with only one head in each pail.

No time is wasted in consuming it! The way they lick the empty pails you are given the impression they would like a second helping.

But good appetites show the farmer that all is well. His concern is the little one that has no desire for food but lies weak and indifferent in a corner.

SO THE Good Shepherd looking over His flock is happy to see those "that hunger and thirst for righteousness", for these are the ones He can satisfy!   Matt. 5:6

Country Style

February 2, 1967

A seed catalog has already arrived. Its colorful shiny pages hypnotize me and wipe away all thoughts of the spading, weeding and watering.

As I pore over its contents, the luscious-looking strawberries, lovely roses and new varieties of glads try to steal my affections. Even the string beans are beautiful.

A person must have a lot of self-control or he will go overboard when he starts filling out the order blank.

HOW TIMES have changed! Today the farmer serves his livestock corn that has been shelled and daintily ground. Time was when the animals had to get it off the cobs themselves.

Those were the days the children had the job of picking up cobs from the feed yards. Nothing went to waste then. These cobs kept the old kitchen stove going.

And that old kitchen stove stirs up warm memories. It was a versatile piece of equipment. Besides cooking and baking, it heated the kitchen.

It was a familiar sight to see someone toasting their feet at its open oven.

It also served as water heater. The tank at one end could be filled with water and the stove would heat it.

Its big flat top was perfect for baking flatbread and lefse.

And when the little pigs got chilled the farmer would set his basket of pigs before the open oven and soon they would be lively again.

The old cook stove was wonderful in its day, but I think I'll settle for just memories of it and enjoy the turn-of-the-dial convenience of my electric stove.

THERE HAVE been some big changes in milking too! It hasn't been long since the farmer (or his wife) balanced on a one-legged stool, snuggled against the cow, and milked "slow motion."

Today the milking machines take care of many cows at a time.

The process of obtaining the milk has changed but the milk remains the same healthful white drink it always has been.

AFTER THE chores of the day are finished the farmer can settle down in his favorite chair, have the thermostat adjusted to his comfort and relax and enjoy himself where blustery weather can't reach him.

And Psalms 91 tells me about a place where I can be cozily sheltered "under His wings."

Country Style

February 9, 1967

A forenoon just doesn't seem right without our morning lunch. When pouring up our coffee I glance out the window and have to smile, for it's apparent we aren't the only ones with this habit.

I see the heads of the junior-sized calves reaching for mouthfuls of hay. With this age-group there is a lot of pushing and shoving at snack-time.

Further down the line I get the rear view of the cows eating around the hay feeder. The orderly way they are lined up, flank to flank, reminds me of people sitting up to a lunch counter.

TAKING IN a farm show isn't just a one-day affair. The farmer sees a lot of interesting new equipment, feeds and seeds there, but the packet of material and advertising he brings along home is food for thought for many a winter night.

At his leisure he can mull over this information and consider its worth. Some of the things he sees and studies may find a place in his plans for the future.

IT'S NEARING Valentines' Day, and on behalf of all the farmers' wives I have a valentine message for the farmer -

"You are rugged and strong as the denim you wear,
But we have seen you brush away a tear at an unexpected gesture of love...or a prayer.
Your keen eyes keep a close watch on crops, machinery and livestock.
But we have caught you enjoying a sunset.
During busy seasons your time is precious.
But we have seen you drop everything to help a neighbor in need.
The dozens of chore gloves you wear out each year are proof of the tough manual labor you do,
But your gentle handclasp sends us a message of love.
After months of hard labor, and the harvest is in,
Our hearts well up within us as we hear you give God the credit.
You growers of food,
Suppliers of vittles to the world.
We are glad you asked us to walk hand in hand with you in your rural domain.
We're proud to be your wives."

VALENTINES relay a message of love. We have been sent a heavenly valentine, decorated with a rainbow, a cross, the "birds of the air" and the "lillies of the field", which all proclaim "He careth for you." Matt. 6:25-30

Country Style

February 16, 1967

These winters days we take advantage of our husbands' free time by getting them to help us with some projects around the house - like manning a paint brush and doing some repair jobs.

Sometimes I have the feeling they wish spring would come so they could get back to their tractors and fields.

THE HOUSEWIFE isn't the only one that has the job of changing bedding. Many times a week the farmer loads up bales of straw and beds down a place for the animals to rest.

There is something special about the feel of fresh bedding that makes the cows so anxious to lay down on it, they can hardly wait until the job is finished.

This clean bedding saves the farmer a lot of cow-scrubbing at milking time.

THE PHEASANTS have turned from the hunted to the hunter as they try to stalk down something to eat. With the snow cover on the fields they even resort to the highways.

Someone ought to warn them that the auto is just as deadly a weapon as a gun!

And the little winter birds are very busy flitting here and there, looking for a morsel or two. I suppose their busyness helps keep them warm.

IT'S CORN-SHELLING TIME! Before daylight is fully here the commotion begins. I can hear the corn-sheller, tractors and trucks getting set up as men and machines take on the job of emptying our two-tiered crib of corn.

The corn ears are fed into the sheller to come out amid whirlwinds of husk, as naked cobs and truckloads of golden kernels.

The deep growl of the corn-sheller lets me know they are still at it, and reminds me the men have to be lunched and fed.

The corn shelling jobs must be done before the warmness of spring causes spoilage in the outside cribs.

Now all that is left of our corn crib is an empty spot in the farmyard and some rolls of corn cribbing. The cobs and husks went into the feed yards for bedding.

I WATCHED the wind carry the cornhusks around and wondered where their wayward journeys would end. It reminded me of Psalm 1 where it says, "The wicked are like the chaff which the wind drives away - but the child of God is like a deeply rooted tree."

Country Style

February 23, 1967

If there's one thing you can't depend on, it's the weather.

Several of Spring's days wandered into February. But it didn't take long for that month to show its true colors. With snow and wind it let us know that it still belonged to Winter.

For one day Nature entertained us. From our windows the world seemed to be a blur. We would gauge the storm by whether we could see anything of our neighbor's grove.

When a snowstorm is brewing the dairyman begins to worry that it will prevent his milk hauler from picking up his milk. The cows keep giving milk whether there is a place to put it or not. But he was glad that this storm was short-lived.

The next day found the thermometer down, but the world and the snow seemed to be at peace again. The sun shining on the rippled landscape made it look like little diamonds had fallen overnight.

Then a little rabbit hopped across the lawn with its powder-puff tail bouncing across the snow, and the school bus went by. Things were back to normal again.

THE FARMER is ten feet tall to the little boys who call him "Daddy." Everything he does is the best! Their one aim in life is to be like him. In their eyes he is a "saint in overalls."

In their toy box you will find miniature tractors and machinery the same color and brand as Dad's. They worship everything from his muscles to his old straw hat. What little boy hasn't tried on Daddy's heavy work shoes and hobbled around in them?

At chores time you will see these little fellows tagging behind like the farmer's shadows. At this age, they have no fear of the machinery or the animals. What Daddy does, they think they can do.

Their eyes absorb everything. You'd be surprised at the knowledge they have about the chores. They can give you all the details.

The blueprint they are forming for their own lives has the exact dimensions of this man they worship and love. At this age there is no question but that they will be farmers too!

Following in Daddy's footsteps they learn many things first hand. They get a peek at responsibility, hard work and honesty from Dad's actions. They pick up his gestures and speech, try to walk with the same swing in their step, and stand with their hands in their pockets like he does. They want to be carbon copies of him.

THESE FEW lines of verse say it so well.

Yea, last night, it snow a heap...
On a level two feet deep.
Daylight time or just before...
I start out to do dem chore.
My boy Gus yell, "Me go too."
I say, "Snow too deep for you."
Right quick he answer back...

(continued)

(February 23, 1967 – continued)

"I can step in Daddy's tracks."
Den his mother pat his head...
"Gude boy, Gus," was all she
    said.
But I know she think lots more
When we start to do dem chore.
"...Little boys walk everyday...
Where the old man leads the
    way...
Better walk straight, like a
    crack...
When boys step in "Daddy's
    tracks."

SEED CORN salesmen are approaching their customers with order blank in hand. More decisions! What varieties and numbers should the farmer gamble this year's harvest results on? When they get to talking about all these seed corn numbers I almost expect someone to call out "bingo".

Numbers are so non-descriptive. When ordering glad bulbs the names give a clue to what to expect...like the elegance of "Elizabeth the Queen" or the neat formation of "Spic and Span". I should think it would be more fun ordering corn if it had names like "Kernel King" or "Corn-crib Champion". But perhaps it would be a problem thinking up that many names: numbers can be mixed into thousands of combinations.

WE LIVE in a world of numbers. There are social security numbers, telephone numbers, license numbers, bank numbers and zip code numbers.

Numbers are so impersonal. Who wants to be known by a social security number? or a bank number? It's so good to be called by your first name.

With millions of people in the world today, how wonderful to be on a first name basis with the One who says, "Fear not, for I have redeemed you; I have called you by name; you are mine."   Isaiah 43:1

Country Style

March 2, 1967

Looks can be deceiving. You would expect "duchess," our pony, to act befitting her regal name. She certainly looks innocent, but she has a few tricks under her shaggy forelocks.

When the cows are eating silage at the feedbunks she knows how to make plenty of room for herself. A few well-placed nips give the cows a lot of respect for her.

She looks out for herself during cold weather by pushing in between the cows to keep warm.

When trying to catch her, she is very coy and elusive. With a toss of her head she uses her best "catch me if you can" manner.

But what wisdom! When a little child is on her back she will behave with greatest care. Yet if, in her estimation a rider is a few pounds too heavy, she can give him a bronco-bucking ride. She has horse-sense plus.

SCIENCE AND farming are progressing so rapidly that the farmer has to spend some time studying up on all these new discoveries. These short courses come with pancake feeds and free dinners. (The farmer likes sausages, but doesn't go for baloney.)

These sprays, fertilizers and new methods must be explained and discussed. Soon a farmer will have to have a doctor's degree to understand what he is doing. But he is well aware that he can't get "100 plus" bushel corn with farming methods of the past.

DECISIONS, decisions, decisions.

Mental gears are busy turning as the farmer attempts to draw up his blueprint for this year's farming operations. Oh, to have some extra-sensory perception about this time! If he knew the rain and weather conditions he could plan accordingly. But that's what makes farming an adventure!

He must have his plans worked out before spring work begins. What he is aiming at is to get the most dollars from each acre.

He must decide what seeds will be best and consider new oat, soybean and seed corn numbers.

How much fertilizer should be put on? This is a weighty decision. A good salesman will tell him it costs to be without it, but he can't help but feel a drain on the pocketbook while he is waiting for the salesman's promises to come true.

He must consider new weed control methods and the new equipment it might involve.

(continued)

(March 2, 1967 – continued)

After all these decisions are made, this blueprint must be put into action. With good management and the necessary sun and rain the farmer "*hopes*" at harvest time to see his blueprint result in a good return for his time and investment. How satisfying for him to be able to say then, "*It worked out pretty much as I planned.*"

GOD HAS a blueprint for every life, worked out in minute detail, for us to follow.

Someday when His harvest is in, what joy it will be to hear Him say as he looks back over our life, "It's just like My plan." Jer. 29:11

Country Style

March 9, 1967

The first part of March is "moving time" for the farmer who is re-locating. This isn't as simple as just packing up the dishes and calling a moving van.

When a farmer moves, he must transport all his machinery, load up his cows, pigs, chickens, cats and dog, and his corn, oats and hay - plus the furniture and household goods.

It's a big job! It takes planing, a lot of strong backs and big trucks.

But it is almost too much when at the close of this big day he has to try to get some order in a strange barn so he can finally get his cows milked. About this time he declares his next move will be to town.

WITH ALL the sickness going around, every little sneeze and sniffle gets the farmer's wife worried. When the farmer gets under the weather she really has problems...like "who is going to do the chores and milk the cows?" She's afraid the answer may be "you!"

WE HAVE a big colorful calendar, thanks to a reader.

It arrived the last days of February so we were able to enjoy February's picture of some golfers against a beautiful Hawaiian background. It is lucky it came as late as it did for I don't know if my farmer could stand to have those golfers tease him for a whole month.

March has a pretty scene from Ireland, an old castle set in lots of green grass and green trees.

With this new calendar it looks like we are going to see the world from our kitchen chairs. That's inexpensive and comfortable traveling! I know I'll enjoy it.

WE HAVE a piece of equipment that makes the barn nice and cozy on chilly days. This portable heater looks like a rocket and can really shoot out the heat. When it is running it roars like a jet warming up.

This makes winter chores a little less unpleasant.

A BLUSTERY howling wind, a house creaking with the cold, and the "crunch", "crunch" as you walk on the snow in zero weather are some of the voices of winter. Soon these sounds will be replaced by the "pitter-patter" of April showers as seasons change.

When the bone-chilling March wind blows, I can warm my heart on this precious thought - "I have loved you with an everlasting love!" that changes not with the weather, or the months, seasons or years. Jer.31:3

Country Style

March 16, 1967

Before we know it, our long work days will be here again and we won't have much time for social life. Remember last fall all the plans we had...to visit the neighbors, make some calls on shut-in and elderly acquaintances, and do some entertaining?

So...we'd better be getting it done!

IN OUR neighborhood last week we had a little variation on that old nursery rhyme "Ding, dong bell," as a heifer fell down into a six-foot hole.

She had assumed a sitting position and looked up into her rescuers' faces. It was rather cramped quarters for such a large animal. The problem was how to get her out alive.

The tractor loader had lots of pull and got her back up and on all four feet again. From the laborious way she hobbled off I would assume this adventure left her with a few aches and pains.

SOME INTERESTING facts: China with its multitudinous population has 80 percent of its work force in agriculture and still comes up short. The United States has less than 10 percent of its manpower on the farm and besides providing for its own needs it sends foodstuffs to the hungry of the world.

I think the American farmer deserves a pat on the back!

A FARMER'S wife has to be "some cooker!" She is accustomed to making coffee by the gallon and preparing food in quantities. She takes "feeding 5 to 6 extra men" in her stride provided she has had plenty of warning.

But I think her most nerve-wracking experiences are the times she is informed in the last minute and finds herself with frozen meat and hungry men.

That really calls for resourcefulness!

THE FARMER is examining his equipment and getting things in good running order before the busy season. Everything has to be ready to go!

Above all, his tractor must be in tip-top shape. If a tune-up, overhaul or repair job is necessary he'd better get it done.

Or maybe he should just trade it off for a new one!

To keep his tractor running efficiently, it must be kept clean and air and oil filters must be replaced, for dirt is the enemy of the tractor engine. A motor can be ruined in one minute when dirt gets into the motor, I am told.

OUR DIRTY and grimy hearts need some overhauling too. For smooth and happy-running lives we can get that needed tune-up by sincerely asking, "Create in me a clean heart, O Lord, and renew a right spirit within me."   Ps. 51:10

Country Style

March 23, 1967

I overheard our calf "chorus" the other day. With the barn door open, I got full benefit of their concert. I didn't realize they could harmonize. They were "bawling" in 3 or 4 parts.

CHICKS, bunnies and eggs.
The store-bought variety are plastic, candy and cardboard, but on the farm you will find the real thing.

A mother hen and her chicks are something you just don't see nowadays. It was a cozy sight to see one settled down in the straw with her little ones peeking out from under her wings.

Now chicks come in quantities from the hatchery and the mother hen has gone out of date.

I SUPPOSE every farmer's wife has tried her hand at raising chicks. At this time of the year we reminisce over those days of excitement, work and worry.

Bringing the baby chicks home from the hatchery was a big event. The chicks came into their new home in big cardboard boxes. It was an enjoyable task to take each little warm ball of fluff out of the box and set it on its two wirey legs. Soon the brooder-house was full of "cheeping chicks", busy using their little beaks to investigate.

They needed very warm quarters. We would have to shed our wraps as we came in the door.

They were delicate creatures in those early days of their life. A drop in temperature would cause them to pile up and smother. Lots of attention and care was required to get them off to a good start, and there always were some losses.

When chicks are brand new to the world they are cuddly and sweet, but as they grow into the feather-stage, taking care of them soon becomes a chore. At least, that's one woman's opinion.

> Little chick,
> Tell me quick,
> What is Easter?
>
> "Yesterday my home
> Was an eggshell tomb,
>   dark
>   confining
>   still
> Where joy was nil.
>
> "Then my tomb broke
> And I awoke
> To a bright day,
>   to run
>   to fly
>   to play
> To New Life!
> That is Easter."

"HE LOVED me and gave Himself for me" are precious words to meditate on during this Holy Week. When they have taken root in the heart there will blossom forth a most glorious Easter morn.

Country Style

March 30, 1967

There came to our farm a balmy day
That bewitched our old cows and made them play.
They kicked up their heels in an unladylike way.
It was their manner of saying, "It's Spring!"

ALMOST EVERY hog house in the country is having a population-increase these days. It is a tense time for the farmer. He hopes for large litters and tries his best to save each little newcomer.

He will spend both day and night in the hog house getting the new arrivals off to a good start. Each pig he saves may mean the difference between profit or loss in his hog business.

The pens are bedded with nice clean straw and the farmer tries to keep his little pigs warm and dry. If they are strong and healthy he usually doesn't have any eating problems. They are pretty good at helping themselves.

He takes great pride in announcing an average of 9 or 10 pigs per sow... But a low average gets his pig-year off to a bad start.

MANY FARM children get into the pig or sheep business when they are given some frail little animal that needs extra care. They faithfully bottle feed it, and often these little ones are kept in a big box in the kitchen so they can keep a close watch on them.

Many unusual things can happen on these projects. On one occasion, in the middle of the night, two little pigs made their usual eating-time commotion. When they received no attention they became impatient, found their way out of their box and came sauntering into the downstairs bedroom.

The lady of the house thought this was going a little too far, and that was the end of their kitchen sojourn.

WIRE BASKETS full of white fresh eggs are a pretty sight. But to those who do the chicken chores this sight means work. For after gathering these hundreds of eggs, there still is the tedious task of packing them into egg crates for the egg man to pick up.

An egg is a fragile thing. What is worse to clean up than a broken egg! And when working with them you can expect a few of these.

WE DON'T have to be afraid of putting all our eggs in one basket when we are using "God's basket" ..."For He who spared not His own Son, will he not also give us all things with Him?"   Rom. 8:32

Country Style

April 6, 1967

God has taken the winter reel of black and white days off his projector and is about to run for us his beautiful technicolor production called "Spring."

Everyone's champing at the bit..."waiting."

Even the little blades of grass are getting impatient. Many of them have already taken a chance on turning green.

The trees are budded and one of these days will burst forth their leaves.

The green 4-bottom plow looks bored setting out in the yard. I'm sure it's anxious to get the grease off its mold-board and show its power in the black earth.

WE ARE ABLE to put a lot more into each day now that the sun is spending more time with us. And there's plenty to do!

The housewife is getting anxious to begin her spring housecleaning. The dirty windows need some sparkle and there's a garden to get at and a lawn to rake.

Farmers have been taking their manure spreaders on trips out to the fields, sort of trial runs to see if the soil is workable. But some of these spreaders have come across soft spots that left them grounded and stuck in the mud. You just can't rush nature.

THE NOON markets are a must for the farmer, especially if he has something to sell. It can either take the joy out of his day or put a smile in it.

Some of these announcers really come up with some hard to understand reports...like bulls selling at fat cattle prices. The cattle feeder finds it hard to figure a profit at those prices - even using new math!

THE BIRDS are back. Every day seems to bring in another southern flight. The robins began to arrive the first day of spring and have been real busy getting settled in our neighborhood. It seems every time I look out the window I see one.

Many birds are picking up twigs, straw and string for the construction work they are doing. When the lawn gets raked they won't have so much material to choose from.

I heard a meadowlark's song, and there it was...sitting in its favorite pose on the fence post. The meadowlark's happy tune is the sweetest sound I know. For years their songs have brightened my washdays. I look forward to hanging up clothes when I can listen to them.

AND THE One who wrote the song for the meadowlark to sing is able to place just as sweet a tune in our hearts!

Country Style

April 13, 1967

At this time of the year if you look twice at the people working in the fields, you'll discover they aren't all men. You will see some farmers' wives in the wagons shoveling oats into the seeder, or riding the tractor, disking or dragging.

Some farm women are just as much at home on a tractor seat as on a car seat. These lucky farmers really got helpmates when they said "I do."

IT'S TIME to get the grain into the ground. The oats has already made its trip through the fanning mill where the weed seeds and chaff were sifted away, and now its ready to go.

When you look at a handful of dry oats it's hard to imagine the hidden life there. These seeds look as lifeless as a pebble or a sliver of wood, but when they are placed in the damp warm earth they become alive and soon turn a whole field into green growth.

This will always be a mystery to me. Living with all these miracles makes the farm an awesome place in spring.

WHAT MAKES a man a farmer?
It isn't his land,
Or his tractor or plow,
Or his overalls, workshoes,
Or lots of "know-how".

It's an intangible thing
That runs through his veins,
That carries him through
The dust storms and rains.

That makes him invest
His money and time
Without a guarantee of
Receiving a dime.

That gives him confidence
With nature to cope.
It's that tender but powerful substance
Called "Hope".

DUALS ARE "in". We have two extra big tires leaning against the barn...all ready to slip on when the tractor gets at the disking and plowing. These promise to give better traction, and won't spin and pack the ground as much as singles.

You really need traction when you get at some of these tough jobs - like disking or plowing up alfalfa.

WHEN we have hard pulling and life seems to be all uphill we can get needed traction by claiming this promise - "Be not dismayed, for I am your God; I will strengthen you, I will help you, I will uphold you with my victorious right hand."   Isa. 41:10

Country Style

April 20, 1967

Plowing time...when the farmer always wishes he had more horsepower so he could show his neighbor he's got a lot of pull.

With one wheel riding in the newly made furrow and the white seagulls following behind, he patiently travels back and forth across his fields. He uses his plow to erase last year's work. It turns under the cornstalks and growth of 1966. When he is finished, his field looks like a clean black slate, ready for new problems, new solutions and new results.

THE EXTENSION Clubs have a community improvement project this year. Many individual clubs are improving their mailboxes and planting flowers by them.

Our box was in sad shape and we decided even flowers wouldn't do a thing for it. So we got a new one. And do you know, even the Post Office Department is happy about it? Now, if the flowers will only grow.

APRIL ON the farm means caring for April babies - the lambs, the kittens and puppies, the calves and pigs. All these animal babies have a helplessness and innocence that endears us to them.

Our latest little ones are two lambs.

When lambs are new, their ears and feet appear too big for their skinny little bodies. Even their skin seems to be a few sizes too large, and it is covered with little kinks and curlicues - not soft wool.

You can just take a look at our lambs and tell if they have been fed or not. When it's time to eat, their little middles are sunken in, but a bottle of milk soon rounds their sides out again.

The first few days of their lives they are very clumsy and have a time getting up on their four wobbly feet. But in about a week they become frolicsome. It's very entertaining to watch their happy goings-on. They seem to grow springs in the bottom of their four feet, and run and jump and bounce up into the air with trampoline-like action. But they look so little and frail to be doing such fancy capers.

ALL THESE little animals on our farm need care and attention. The little lambs are bottle fed three times a day. On school day mornings I hear this request, "Remember to feed my lambs." So I play nursemaid and bring them their noon feeding.

And then I am reminded of a request the Good Shepherd made - "Lovest thou me? Then feed MY lambs."   John 21:15

Country Style

April 27, 1967

Today HORSEPOWER isn't really horse power.

The old workhorse is gone...but not entirely forgotten. I'm sure many people have memories of some faithful "King", "Barney" or "Lady".

The modern "farm workhorse" isn't dapple gray but comes in bright colors of green, orange and red. It runs on duals and is loaded with power. This tractor can turn more furrows in an hour than slow horsepower could in a day.

The day's work of these old workhorses was limited. The farmer of yesterday had to spend time feeding, currying and harnessing his horses. When the team came home all sweaty from a hard morning in the field, he would have to water and feed them and then give them the needed hour's rest before hitching them up again.

Now with his gas-eating workhorse, the farmer just fills it up, crawls on the seat and he's ready to go. The tractor will keep going around the clock and not mind it a bit.

But you could love a horse! This modern machine may outdo the patient horse in many ways...but it can't nose a sugar lump! And who would care to pat a tractor's rear?

IN DAYS past a horse was a necessity, but today a horse is a luxury. In the past, horse collars, fly nets, bridles and reins, tugs and doubletrees were familiar items. Today the horseshoe is about all that is left of the horse era.

Did you know that the game of horseshoes is becoming popular again? We have our stakes in the ground and during spare time you can hear the "clink-clank" as someone practices up.

SOMETIMES sad things happen on the farm. Our puppies were getting big enough to be a nuisance. They could find more things to drag on the lawn. Some of these things would have been better off buried. But it was hard to be angry when three friendly furry fat short-legged things came eagerly running to you for love and attention.

Then one morning there was only one! The highway had claimed two more lives. The little survivor is pretty lonesome.

SPRING flowers give the most joy for the least effort. And there aren't many flowers that can out-dazzle the colorful tulip.

My Tulip Patch

The Creator, feeling gay,
Took His paintbrush out one day.
He splashed and dabbed the
   colors bright
...for my delight!
Cinderellas of the sod,
Clothed by the wand of God.

SPRING CALLS for an attitude of trust. The farmer must have faith to begin again and be willing to place another year of his labor into God's hands for His blessing.

"I know not what the future hath of marvel or surprise, ...I only know I cannot drift beyond His love and care."

Country Style

May 4, 1967

Spring is everywhere. The ground is carpeted with green velvet, the willows have the yellow-green leaves of Spring, puffy clouds drift across the blue sky...and we trip over purple violets in the grass.

Like an adolescent who is both child and adult, April turned out to be a confused mixture of winter and summer.

She behaved like a little child throwing a tantrum as she huffed and puffed across the plowed fields, chasing everything in her path, and leaving woven wire fences decorated with cornhusks, and the ditches lined with dirt drifts...and our windowsills covered with fine dirt.

Then the temperature fell as she reverted back to winter.

WE HAVE been sympathizing with our 4-H yearling ewe, who lost her warm 12 lb. coat when she was sheared just before the last chilly spell.

I'm sure she really noticed the change in temperature. We took our winter jackets out again, but the poor sheep could do nothing but shiver!

WHEN THE farmers begin planting corn I know it's time to get the glad bulbs in the ground. It's a 90-day wait from planting time till blooms. Every year there are some new colors to try. I'm always anxious to see if they will be as pretty as the pictures advertising them.

Have you ever noticed how easy it is to order nursery stock and seeds, but when it arrives, what an effort it is to get it into the ground?

DURING THE winter, wildlife has taken over the farmer's property. Now that he is working in the field he disturbs and scares up foxes, rabbits, pheasant and other small animals. Sometimes he has to take time out from his plowing to do a little fox hunting.

He soon discovers this sly quick animal didn't get his crafty reputation for nothing!

The alfalfa and oat fields are getting green. The farmer is eager to see how his hay fields made it through the winter. He doesn't like to see bare spots. A good stand will bring him many bales of hay.

So the Sower goes forth to sow the Word and waits to see if it will grow. A good stand will bring Him much fruit - a hundredfold, sixty fold, or thirty fold.   Matt. 13:3-9

Country Style

May 11, 1967

It's time for the return of the barn swallows. Each year as they show up, I am reminded of my Grandfather, who every spring awaited their return before he would plant his corn.

The swallows make themselves at home in the barn, build their nests under the rafters and perch on the electric wires.

THE FARMER has been busy picking up the bags of seed corn he ordered. This can get to be quite a job if he succumbed to every seed corn salesman. Now he has to get his corn planter out and begin planting these kernels.

Farming keeps changing. Every year the farmer aims for bigger corn yields. To increase last year's crop, some farmers are planting narrow rows this Spring. Whether to change from 40 inch to 30 inch rows has been a hot topic for debate. The trouble with these new ideas is that they cost money, for narrow rows call for machinery to fit - a new planter, cultivator and harvester.

TO MOMS - young, old or middle-aged...and especially one in particular!

"For your care when I was wee
And lullabies upon your knee,
Thank you, Mom.

"For your sacrifice and cheers
Through childhood years,
Thank you, mom.

"For your love...an unseen force
That kept me on the upward
  course,
Thank you, mom.

"Although words cannot repay.
Accept this "thank-you Mom"
  bouquet,
God bless you, Mom!"

Mother love is the same, whether it is found in the city or the country. It is always priceless. So often we take it for granted, but at this time of the year we stop to take a better look at it...and thank God for it!

Mother Love
It started out so simply...
    with a tiny baby in her arms,
      and diapers,
      two o'clock feedings
      and lullabies.
As her child grew, this love grew.
    And she gave of herself-
      her lap was claimed by this
        little fellow,
      her kisses served as
        medication for both
        heart and body hurts,
      her time was not her own.
She didn't know how binding this
    tie had become until he
    reached boyhood
And she found this life was part of
    herself-
      she felt pain at his pain,
      joy at his happiness,
      grief at his disobedience.

(continued)

(May 11, 1967 - continued)

Then it was time for him to walk
  alone
 and she showed him what he
  could be;
 her encouragement boosted him
  upward,
 her prayers guided and
  strengthened him,
 her faith in him never faltered.
Now he is a man...
 and her love has become a
  magnet with an invisible hold,
  that neither party can break.
 And her love and prayers will
  follow her child even after she
   is gone.
- For a mother's love and influence
has no end!

  THERE IS One who loves and
gives more than any Mother...and
how Mothers need what He has to
give!   Jer. 31:3

Country Style

May 18, 1967

The wind has been the main topic of conversation this spring. This windy weather affects both livestock and humans, and has been pretty hard on trees and plants too.

It makes working in the fields more tiring than usual...and dirtier. These black-faced characters that come in for meals are not members of a minstrel show...but our dirt-blown husbands. All that is missing is a top hat, cane and banjo. With their white rimmed eyes (from their goggles) peering out of their dust-covered faces, you can hardly recognize them. But soap and water make them familiar again.

These forceful gusts of wind irritate the livestock and make them nervous. It was a good thing we were around one windy Sunday when the restless cattle broke a gate and headed off with the wind at their backs in stampede fashion. They didn't get far.

I GUESS we are all fed up with the wind now, but I can remember days when we wished and looked for a breeze to get the windmill turning.

That was before the electric motor was used to pump water, and the wind was depended on to fill the stock tank for thirsty livestock. Today the windmill is just a piece of scenery, its usefulness out-dated!

THE NEW time has its compensations. It makes it easier to take in crack-of-the-dawn events like sunrises and all of nature's "good mornings!" We discover it is a special time of day.

The mourning doves gently awaken the world with their melancholy cooing...which is much better than a rooster's sharp reveille. The mourning doves are such trusting, peaceful birds it is hard to believe the talk about having open season on them.

FROM THE way the hoppers and tanks of fertilizer have been going down the road en route to farms, our community should be having some bumper crops come fall - provided we get the necessary rainfall.

Every farmer must be feeding his soil this spring. The soil needs supplements just as our bodies need food to grow and live. But this soil food is pretty expensive, and makes the grocery bills look like chicken feed.

BUT, HOW wonderful to find satisfying food and drink that is abundant...and free!

"Ho, every one who thirsts, come to the water; and he who has no money, come, buy and eat!" Isaiah 55:1.

Country Style

May 25, 1967

These past weeks the farmer has had one thing on his mind - "Get the corn planted!" Morning, noon and night he has been moved by this compulsion.

After the field is prepared, the planter gets its seasonal workout. Gauged to the correct planting depth, its four planter shoes make neat tracks back and forth across the black soil, while the long marker makes a new path for the next trip across.

The planter's hoppers are filled and refilled with seed corn and soil insecticide for rootworm. Approximately $5 worth of seed corn and insecticide drops into the ground every acre the planter travels.

A farmer takes great pride in straight rows...much like a seamstress' pride in her straight seams. Some farmers still check their corn. Then each kernel is clicked off by the planter wire at exact intervals so when it comes up, the field can be cross-cultivated. But the majority of farmers today either hill drop or drill their corn. And with contour farming, its beauty is not in its straight rows, but in its graceful curves.

When the planter has finished with the corn, the soybeans will be waiting.

I GUESS "the chores" are the straws that just about break the farmer's back. He is anxious to put in as much time as possible in the field, but the chores are always waiting at the beginning and ending of every day. He has to take time out to haul some hay, grind feed and do some cleaning besides the milking and feeding.

After rushing through two or three hours of chores in the morning he says it feels good to sit down on the tractor and relax.

OUR TWO lamb orphans are growing, both in weight and appetite. I believe they would drink milk until they burst.

Did you know that selfishness shows up even in the sheep family? The little black-faced lamb always finishes its bottle first, and then persistently tries to get what is left of the other lamb's lunch. And scolding doesn't help!

A "BEAUTIFUL DAY IN MAY" cannot be wasted indoors. We've had too few of them. So we find tasks that will bring us outside - working on the lawn, washing windows, hanging up clothes or tending the garden. Here under a blue cloud - decorated sky our ears and eyes grab the free delights that come on a day in May when the temperature is just right, and the breeze is lazy. Our hearts are full as we pack these treasures inside.

We cannot help but feel the hand of God in His happy universe with the many birds singing praises in each its own inimitable way, the white violet faces smiling in their humble corner, and the beautiful iris exhibiting His intricate workings. Then our hearts too must join Nature in singing His praises.

"The Lord reigneth; let all the earth rejoice!"   Ps. 97:1

Country Style

June 1, 1967

School days are over for another year. The country school has been vacated after another nine-month session of activity and playground noise. Now its doors and windows are tightly closed and it seems to be quietly resting. With the talk of reorganization, its life may be almost over.

But these rural school houses hold many memories. Here several generations have learned reading, writing and arithmetic. They had their advantages and their disadvantages.

Outside many of these schools there still stands an old pump and outdoor-type restrooms as reminders of earlier days. The heating facilities of the past weren't modern either. Then the teacher had to get to school early in order to start the fire and have the room warm.

And in those days taxpayers didn't have to spend thousands of dollars to build gymnasiums, because the kids got all the exercise they needed by walking miles to and from school. They walked along, swinging their old tin syrup-can lunch pail. Sometimes they dawdled along the way, playing in mud puddles or snow drifts, or picking wild flowers.

But, today most of these schools have modern facilities. Each country school is like one big family, with the older students looking after the little ones. The rural school teacher is more than a classroom teacher. She is principal, school nurse, musical director, athletic coach...and janitor!

This is her little family and she usually takes them under her wings, helping where each needs help, and encouraging them scholastically and trying to make good citizens of them.

Three cheers for the old country school...where each individual was important, where the love for learning took root and grew in eager minds, where there usually were just enough pupils to make a good ball team and where the girls became almost as good ball players as the boys.

The old country school has filled a need and served well through the years. Those of us who have attended these rural schools can honestly say we're thankful for these memories and feel it didn't hurt us a bit!

THE RURAL schools still have the end-of-the-year school picnic, which includes the families of the district. Each family comes with a bountiful lunch basket, and there are ball games, visiting...and eating!

The excited children look forward to this event because it is the beginning of vacation.

ON MAY 30 we observed Memorial Day. For most of us it was a memory day. We came to these quiet places with our hands full of bouquets and our hearts full of memories...of a little child that didn't stay very long with us...of dear mothers, fathers or grandparents that had finished their tasks here on earth...of other loved ones that had made our life richer for having known them...and also of the men who fought to keep our country free. These people are gone but not forgotten.

On this day we could not help but be reminded of the fragility of our own lives, yet this carries no fear when we know the Good Shepherd-

"Yea, though I walk through the valley of the shadow of death, I will fear no evil...for Thou art with me." Ps. 23:4

Country Style

June 8, 1967

Now it has been revealed! The world can see what the farmer has been planning and doing. A design has been coming out of these black fields. At first, faint green stripes appeared that each day became bolder and more definite. Some fields have a checkered pattern, and contoured fields have a distinctive design of their own.

As we drive along the countryside it is interesting to discover what the farmer has planted. The solid rows indicate soybeans and the spaced slim leaves tell us corn is coming up there.

The farmer can't hide his mistakes any longer either, for now the whole world can see if he missed a row or two, or if his rows are crooked.

IT WAS SO good last week to see some puddles again. These much appreciated and waited for raindrops were really pennies from heaven. They improved the scenery, making the lawns green again, gave the seeds laying in the ground a boost - and also improved the dispositions of the farmers!

Rain is the ingredient necessary to a successful farm year that the farmer cannot supply. This he depends entirely on his Partner to provide. He just has to leave it in His hands.

THE COWS are living in the lap of luxury. After spending the winter in the barnyard and eating dry hay and silage and laying on the hard ground or cement, they are spending these days in green pastures. Here there is tender fresh grass to eat and a carpet of grass to lay on.

When they are hungry they don't even need to get up, but can just stretch their necks and bite off a mouthful.

Every morning they stand at the gate waiting. The cows look forward to getting out in the pasture as much as children getting out for recess. The barnyard has lost its appeal after having tasted the green pastures.

AND SO it is with us.

"He makes me to lie down in green pastures. He leads me beside still waters; He restores my soul."

Ps. 23: 2,3

That is really living.

Country Style

June 15, 1967

Weddings, anniversaries and showers. June is that time of the year. It was on a day in June when my farmer took a wife, and I began my life as a "farmer's wife."

As we celebrated again, I found myself with a thankful heart, admitting that being a farmer's wife was a rich life - not money-rich, but with the riches of nature, friends, family and home. Money cannot buy happiness like that!

June also is dairy month, when we stop to salute the faithful cow.

Ode to the Cow

"Fountain of nourishment" for the human race,
For thirty days we'll sing your praise.
Your products are Nature's convenience foods -
Fresh, fast, fun...and oh, so good!

Your four white streams each morning and night
Are the old man's sustenance and the baby's delight!
You would never dream what we do with your cream...
It's whipped and frozen for desserts so supreme.

We'll have to acknowledge there's no other spread
To compare with your golden butter on bread.
And many a complimented cook will say, "...Oh,
I always bake with butter, you know!"

Brick and cottage and cheddar cheese
Are tasty nutrients that please.
Now, old faithful dairy cow,
It's time to take a well-deserved bow!

THE FARMERS are busy spraying their fields, fighting the age-old battle against weeds.

And we keep fighting our battles with the weeds in our personal lives.

The farmer gets rid of his with 2-4-D.

We can use I John 1:9: "If we confess our sins, he is faithful and just to forgive our sins, and to cleanse from all unrighteousness."

Country Style

June 22, 1967

What is so neat and prim as a field that has just been cultivated? I have discovered that the farmer has some of the meticulous urges that we find in a housewife.

About this time he is trying to get all his dirty green fields cleaned up...and it bothers him if work gets ahead of him. He is very busy riding his equipment back and forth across his fields, tidying them up.

A clean field with nice black strips between the rows gives him the same feeling of satisfaction that we get when our floors shine, the windows sparkle and everything is in its place.

IT'S FUNNY how a word, a name or a song can open up a whole compartment of memories that we had forgotten all about...like a key opening a treasure chest.

At a concert recently the Norwegian fun song "A Kjore Vatten, a Kjore Ved" (Haul the water and haul the wood!) opened up many happy childhood memories for me.

When I was a little girl, people had homemade entertainment, and no TV. My Dad used to sing this song as one of his children bounced on his knee or rode horsey-style on his foot. I hadn't heard it for years. It reminded me of the happy times we had with all of his Norwegian ditties, and it has been fun reminiscing.

WE JUST observed Father's Day and those of us who are left with only memories of our Dads discovered that the things we remembered were when Dad gave us his time and personal attention - whether it was playing ball with us, taking us fishing, or on a family vacation, or telling us bedtime stories.

This gives us an important clue for these days when we are manufacturing memories for our children.

WITH ALL the tornado watch warnings out recently, there have been many evenings when we have gone to bed rather apprehensively...but each morning we have awakened safe and sound.

One morning we discovered that while we were sleeping, a twister of some kind ripped off part of the roof of the hog house, leaving the building at a leaning angle with pieces of metal and shingles scattered all over, even up on the windmill.

This little wrecker moved only about 150 feet from where we were asleep and we couldn't help but say "thank you" to the One who watches over us both day and night.

"He will not let your foot be moved; he who keeps you will not slumber."   Ps. 121:3

Country Style

June 29, 1967

These last weeks the farmer has been trying to make hay while the sun shines, but the sun has been playing peek-a-boo with him. Yet you won't hear him complain; he remembers too well the dust.

He'll probably tell you this will be some of the cleanest hay he has ever had because it has been washed so many times.

In Norway they have a moisture problem too, but there they hang their hay on the fences to dry.

People have been making hay for centuries but the methods keep changing.

"Conditioning" hay is the latest. Mowing, raking and tenderizing the alfalfa stalks are done in one operation. The cows really go for it! To them there is just as much difference between a conditioned hay bale and an ordinary hay bale as we find between a tough steak and a tenderized one.

THE FOURTH of July is just around the corner! Let's disprove the talk that patriotism is on the wane by saying or doing something that day to exhibit our love for our country. Fly the flag. Tell someone what "the land of the free and brave" means to you. Thank God for the privilege of living in America.

Patriotism Barometer

Do you still get a thrill. . .
when you sing the National
    Anthem?
Are you emotion-prone...
when Old Glory's flown?
Do you glow inside with pride...
when its men march side by side?
Do you daily offer prayer...
for your native land so fair?

A REGULAR circus act was performed in the barn the other night...but neither man nor beast enjoyed it.

As the cows were being tied, a heifer suddenly got the urge to leave. The bottom half of the barn door was closed but this didn't hinder her. She had probably heard the tale of the cow that jumped over the moon and felt she could surely make it over half a barn door.

She forgot that she was weighed down with about five gallons of milk...and her high jump was unsuccessful. She landed on the door with her front legs dangling outside and the rest of her inside. The door swung back and forth a few times and then down crashed cow, door and all.

The onlookers were relieved to discover her good condition and aside from being a little shook up and unnerved it hasn't interfered with her morning and evening delivery of milk.

JUNE BUGS...those dark brown, hard-shelled nuisances that go with summer! They make themselves scarce during the day, but when night comes and the lights go on you can hear them tapping against the windows.

Those big clumsy bugs are very good at putting on a bombardment around the porch lights. But you have to say this much for them...they aren't blood-thirsty like the mosquito.

(continued)

(June 29, 1967 – continued)

THE FARMER almost needs a road map when he comes to cultivating his contoured fields. It is like traveling in a maze that sometimes leaves him in a dead end. Only the person who planted the field really knows where the curving rows will end.

OFTEN OUR LIVES are a series of dark winding passages that make us wonder how things will all come out. But there are no dead ends when we follow the Good Shepherd...for "He knoweth the way I take." Job: 23:10

Country Style

July 6, 1967

A pair of swallows left the ghettos of the barn and have determined to move in on our front porch. They are very messy neighbors as they keep building with their dabs of mud.

And we don't like their belligerent attitude. When we get near they swoop down at us.

I understand other people are having this same problem and have used mothballs to discourage the birds. We'll have to give that a try because we don't appreciate this kind of integration.

THE SOUNDS of hammering and sawing have been coming from the direction of the hog house as the carpenters are busy repairing the storm damage. What the wind did in seconds is taking days to repair.

But we are thankful that it is repairable.

EVERYWHERE we turn there is beauty. On a drive along the countryside we can just feast on the eye-pleasing scenes. A creek's crooked path through a green pasture, contented animals enjoying life, the trees' reflections in the waters...you can not buy lovelier paintings.

The oats are headed and these green fields are attractive as they ripple in the breeze.

There is even beauty in the weeds. Along the roadside the pink wild roses are blooming. You can see them peeking out here and there. You may notice the pretty purple flowers of the wicked thistle. Of all weeds this thistle with its sharp prickles is the most hated by the farmer...and the hardest to get rid of.

AS THE farmer works in his fields these days he has learned to stay out of the low spots. More than one tractor has become imbedded in the mud. When it is loaded down with a cultivator it becomes almost an impossible job to get it out of the mire. The more he works, the deeper it sinks...and his field gets all dug up.

Sometimes as a last resort he has to call out a tow truck or a caterpillar.

It's good to feel solid ground under the tractor wheels. Being stuck in the mud is a hopeless and frustrating feeling.

A SIMILAR PICTURE is painted in these words..."He drew me up from the desolate pit, out of the miry bog, and set my feet upon a rock, making my steps secure." Ps. 40:2

Country Style

July 13, 1967

The 4th of July is over...and the family dog has come out of hiding again. Most dogs turn into cowards when the firecrackers begin to pop.

Poor Pepper, cowering and trembling, tried to move in the house with us, but when we acted inhospitable she had to find another refuge.

Many families spent the 4th holding reunions and picnics. The croquet set was hauled out; the big white coffeepot was kept full of hot coffee; the kiddies were in high gear; and the mothers (as well as the dogs) were relieved when all the firecrackers were gone.

"KNEE-HIGH by the 4th" is the measuring stick the farmer uses to judge his corn's progress. The majority of the corn this year stood up to this measurement.

Now the farmer is rushing to get it laid by before the corn is too big for cultivation.

THIS PAST week the dark green color of the oat fields has become a slightly lighter green. This means that harvest is just around the corner.

Some of the silage wagons are beginning to roll as oat silage time is here. About this time of the year the silos are getting empty, so many farmers use their oat fields for silage.

These days the farmer is so busy with field work that the farmer's wife (or daughter) has to be errand-boy, chauffeur, and what-have-you. She must make trips to town for repairs and supplies, keep an eye on the livestock, taxi the men home for meals and bring them lunch.

Farming is a family-affair, and it's good to feel needed.

THERE ARE so many, many jobs to be done all at once that the farmer is cramming about two days' work into every 24 hours. Daylight Savings Time allows him an after-supper workday. You will find most of the farmers going full speed from dawn's dark till evening darkness sets in.

This busy routine almost makes him feel like he is on a treadmill. After a day of chores, hours on the tractor seat or handling hundreds of bales, he reaches evening weary and ready for rest...and dreams of someone saying, "Take a week off!"

BUT IT is no dream when our tired and troubled hearts hear welcome words - "Come to me, all who labor and are heavy-laden, and I will give you rest" (Matt.12:28). Who can turn down hospitality like that?

Country Style

July 20, 1967

I picked a bouquet of purple clover (those ball-shaped bee-favorites) and set them in a little vase on our kitchen table. They made a cozy bouquet.

And they brought back little-girl-day memories...when we would lie on the grass on a summer day, watch the clouds float across the sky and pull the clover blooms apart and suck out the honey. In those days Nature entertained us well.

Things to enjoy now are day-lilies and daisies, the scent of sweet clover and freshly cut hay, and pert old-fashioned hollyhocks.

THE SPRING pigs are making pigs of themselves. It seems like their self-feeders are always empty. At all hours of the day and night we hear the self-feeders banging. The pigs even have their midnight snacks; the one aim of their life is to keep their stomachs full.

You can't expect the little pigs to grow up to be anything but hoggish and selfish when the big pigs set them that kind of an example.

One warm day two old fat sows were having a noisy argument in the pigyard, and punctuating it with bloodcurdling "oinks." Finally one gave up and walked away. The point of argument seemed to be the wet spot by the water fountain. I can still see the victor plunk her big 500 pounds down on the wet floor. There she lay, enjoying "her" spot and wallowing in her selfishness.

She didn't care that she blocked the water fountain for the other pigs, nor was she ashamed of the bad example she had set for the little pigs who looked on. Pigs will be pigs!

Treatise on Tails

Tails were made for days like these
When flies molest and mosquitoes tease.
For swinging action they're a dandy.
(The cow's flyswatter is always handy.)
But it's hard for the farmer to hold his tongue
When a dirty tail in his face is flung!

THE GALLON water jug is necessary equipment these days. When the farmer is working and sweating out in the sun he needs plenty of water to quench his thirst. And nothing satisfies like cold water on a hot day!

Thirst is common to both man and beast. These summer days the cows make many trips from the pasture to the water fountain.

The dog gets thirsty too. She comes panting to us, her tongue hanging out - a real pathetic picture of thirst!

Our souls get thirsty too – "As the deer pants for streams of water, so my soul pants for you, O God."   Ps. 42:1

Country Style

July 27, 1967

My first glad is in bloom. It is a dainty pink called "Friendship." The first glad, the first rose, the first strawberry and the first tulip always give us a special joy. They introduce us to a new season of bloom that we have been waiting and watching for.

OUR GANG, armed with corn knives and hoes, have been marching up and down the soybean avenues causing mayhem to sunflowers, cockleburs, milkweed and volunteer corn. It takes a lot of work to have a bean field that the farmer can be proud of.

In this day of modern machines there should be an easier way to get rid of this unwanted growth. Trudging up and down the field with a hoe seems almost as old-fashioned as walking behind a plow!

But soybeans are too delicate to stand ordinary weed sprays. The only spray that can be used is too expensive for most farmers, and not entirely satisfactory.

THE GOLDEN grain fields will soon turn to stubble. As you drive along the highway you will see windrowers already making their rounds, and leaving behind them swaths of cut grain.

OUR neighborhood was on the trail of a fugitive last week. The object of all the commotion was a day-old calf that had become frightened and had run into a cornfield.

The corn was too tall and the calf too small...so a vigilante group was formed and the whole cornfield was combed. But, to their dismay...no calf!

As a last resort, a check was made of the pasture again, and I guess the calf's sixth sense had brought it back.

There were some pretty disgusted kids. "All that tramping for nothing!"

COOKING IS an effort on warm days, yet good nutritious meals are needed more now when the men are working hard then at any other time of the year.

And it's almost impossible to keep the cookie jar full. In the summertime cookies disappear quickly, with the children out of school, and with the morning and afternoon lunches (plus a few in between).

But we'll have to admit it's worth the effort of enduring a hot oven. It's fun to notice how the aroma of baking cookies teases everyone who comes in the house. The cookies, cooling on the counter, tempt everyone to sample them.

We get paid by the *'mmmm's'* as one taste usually calls for another.

WE NEVER really know how good anything is until we sample it. Then we want more!

"O taste and see that the Lord is good." Ps. 34:8.

Country Style

August 3, 1967

Pigs in the petunias! And the dog in the nasturtiums!

Raising flowers is a struggle...especially on the farm. There are weeds and lack of moisture to contend with-plus the pigs and the dog.

My pink petunia bed has really been blooming this summer. Its bright blooms have greeted me every time I stepped outside.

Then one night when we were gone for a few hours the little pigs got out. They headed for the house to see how things were over here, and had a party in my petunias. They uprooted the plants and left the bed a section of loose black dirt. It was almost enough to make a person cry!

This is one of the risks we take when we have pigs for such close neighbors.

And the dog likes the cool damp ground in my nasturtiums. I guess I can't really blame her for lying there because I stole her favorite resting place when I dug it up and planted nasturtiums there.

IT SEEMS strange not to be harvesting. But it is a relief. This year our oat field went into the silo.

Harvesting has really changed. Not too many years ago the grain was shocked. A field of neatly arranged golden shocks is scenery that I miss.

At threshing time these bundles were loaded. The hayracks filled with bundles stood in line like grocery carts waiting to be checked out at the supermarket. Then they were unloaded into the big threshing machine. Out came wagon-loads of oats and a big pile of shiny straw.

I think threshing time was harder on the farmer's wife than on the bundle haulers. She usually had to hire someone to help her, or exchange help with a neighbor. It was quite a job to feed a dozen men lunches and dinner. And they expected pie for dessert!

It was usually during the hottest days of the summer that she had to do all this baking and cooking. And on a cook stove! Sometimes she had to feed this crew 3 or 4 days or more.

How happy she was when the combine came along and she had only a couple extra men for meals! By then her cooking was done on an electric or gas stove.

Things have really been looking up for the farmer's wife!

HARVEST TIME. Now the little grains of oats have gone a complete cycle. This spring they were taken out of the bin and planted. They grew and multiplied, are being harvested and will be put into the oat bin again. Some will be fed and some will be saved for next spring's planting.

The completion of this cycle reminds us that God's promise has again come true-

"While the earth remaineth, seed time and harvest, and cold and heat, and summer and winter, and day and night shall not cease."

Gen. 8:22

Country Style

August 10, 1967

4-H'ers are busy sewing in zippers, stuffing their families with practice banana bread, currying calves, trimming hooves and doing a variety of duties.

The high light of the 4-H year is just around the corner. Achievement Days always gets here before we know it. Each year there is the annual scramble to meet the deadline.

Many 4-H'ers are trying to teach big headstrong calves who is boss. Training a calf "to lead" often requires the help of Dad. More than one 4-H'er has needed the help of the whole family to get his run-away calf rounded up again.

If we could get all the behind-the-scene experiences the 4-H'ers are having as they make preparations for Achievement Days we would have a very interesting book.

IT'S FASCINATING to watch the big combines work. These expensive pieces of equipment represent an investment of around $10,000. They have just about finished their oat-jobs for another season. After a rest they will get at the soybean harvest.

The combine's giant appetite.
Isn't content with just a bite.
It licks the windrows off the ground.
Digests them with a growling sound.
When its hopper can hold no more.
It spits out the oats on the truck bed floor.

THE CORN has tasseled. These tall plumes announce that ears are forming and that now would be a good time for some rain.

The stalks of corn stand like royalty with tassel tiaras on their heads. They bundle their little heirs in silk.

When the breeze blows through the field they wave their leaves like a cheering crowd at a ball game.

These tall green fields of corn are the farmer's bank. This is his green stuff! For many months now he has been making deposits of his time and substance into them. He hopes that this bank is sound so when fall comes he'll be able to withdraw his investment- plus some dividends.

THERE IS one bank that will never fail. Our deposits are safe in there.

"But lay up for yourselves treasures in heaven where neither moth nor rust doth corrupt, and where thieves do not break through nor steal. For where your treasure is, there will your heart be also."

Matt. 6:20,21

Country Style

August 17, 1967

Restless August, what's your hurry?
Across the calendar page you scurry.
You rush us through the harvest time;
Your metronome goes double time.

Put some elastic in your days.
We don't like your impatient ways.
Sweet corn. Canning. Vacation fun.
For once we'd like them leisurely done.

For when we say "good-bye" to you,
School days arrive, summer is through!

WHEN THE thermometer soars, we all become uncomfortable. But the heat bothers hogs even more! Too much heat could be the end of a big sow.

Hogs give off 70 to 80 percent of their excess body heat by breathing (not sweating). At 100 degrees a hog must "pant" 20 times as hard as at 80 degree temperatures.

The children always are quick to offer their solution for relief from the heat..."go to the swimming pool."

The farmer tries to offer his big sows some relief by using water too - turning the hose or sprinkler on them. Many farmers have big ventilating fans going to keep their hogs cool.

NO MATTER how tired the farmer is, at chores time he climbs up into the hot silo and scoops down silage for his livestock. He wouldn't dream of letting any of his livestock go without food and water.

He is responsible for them. It matters to him about them.

AND WE ARE not left to our own resources.

"It matters to Him about you!"

Country Style

August 24, 1967

Corn on the cob! With melted butter running down the chin and a pair of teeth sunk into its golden kernels, the expression on the face of the eater is one of pure enjoyment.

The sweet corn season is awaited by everyone. But it is so short. We have only a few days to enjoy it and to get the corn into the freezer.

This year a four-legged robber roamed our patch and we didn't know who would end up with the most corn. Somewhere there is a sweet-corn-fed coon wandering around.

Freezing corn is a time-consuming job and a messy one, but when the family declares store-bought frozen corn can't compare with our own, and then offers to help, we have no choice.

THIS WEEK many farmers are trying to get in a few day's vacation before school starts. This is the first and last chance for many of them. Those with 4-H'ers couldn't go last week, and before that, most farmers were busy with harvest and haying.

It is good to be away from the chores, the fields and the machinery for a few days and relax in another environment. After being gone for a while, home always looks so much better. Then it is even good to see the cows and dog again.

ACHIEVEMENT Days are now only memories. They were days of work, tension, excitement and fun. ...When pigs and calves got more baths than their owners. ...When a little purple piece of ribbon brought tears of joy because it was a ticket to State Fair, and a check from the calf sale brought tears of sadness because it meant parting with a pet.

Our 4-H'ers, their families and some of their projects are back home again. It was a week when the whole family spent more time at the 4-H grounds than at home, lived on hamburgers, pop and pie, and canceled all other engagements.

DURING Achievement Days a well-done project (dress, cookie, sheep, calf or article of handicraft) was admired - but the owner who cared for and worked on the project got the honor and glory.

WE ARE God's "projects"...
"Let your light so shine before men, that they may see your good works - and glorify your Father which is in heaven."   Matt. 5:16

Country Style

August 31, 1967

The farmer is getting curious about his corn crop. You may notice him making trips into his fields, peeking at the corn ears. He is anxious to find out if he will have nubbins or filled-out ears.

It is the very same curiosity that we have when we bake a cake. We often have to peek in the oven to see if the cake is rising satisfactorily. We are anxious to know if it will turn out alright.

There is nothing more the farmer can do to increase or improve his crop. He has done his part - the fertilizing, planting, cultivating and weed-spraying. Now he has to maintain an attitude of "waiting."

MANY RURAL schools are back in the "nine-to-four" routine again. These past weeks there has been scrubbing, window-washing painting and floor polishing going on so these rooms would wear a welcome look for the back-to-schoolers.

Boys and girls, equipped with new shoes and a new lunch pail, were both reluctant and excited as a new school year began. Now teachers are trying to get them settled down to serious study again.

**Sunny sunflower, superbloom...
High above the fields you loom.**

YOU WILL not catch the farmer admiring these butter-colored flowers. He knows them by another name - *weeds*!

But sunflowers aren't hated by everyone. In the country of Turkey, fields of these yellow flowers are grown and the seeds used for bread. And youngsters take a liking to them and become adept at eating their salted seeds.

All spring and summer the Midwest farmer has been fighting sunflowers. He cultivated and sprayed for weeds yet some plants always manage to sneak by. Now their laughing faces taunt him as if they say, "You tried to get rid of me, but I made it anyway!"

Soon these flowers will go to seed and make next year's sunflower battle harder than ever.

If left out of control, sunflowers choke the planted crop and cut down the productiveness of the field.

"DOUBTS" ARE like glittering sunflowers that spring up and make our life of faith a field of confusion. We have to battle them just as the farmer does his weeds.

I Tim. 6:12 - "Fight the good fight of faith."

Country Style

September 7, 1967

Many farmers are taking off a day or two to see the fair. The farmer's wife has discovered that the main attraction isn't the prize cattle, hogs or sheep. We have found that they spend most of their time on "machinery row." There they look over all the changes and improvements in all the machinery lines.

As the farmer spreads out and farms more land he becomes interested in bigger machinery, and machinery that does many jobs in one trip.

The implement companies change and improve their equipment each year just like the dress designers come out with new styles. The Ladies want the latest. So do the farmers!

CHANGE OF SEASONS

Soon our eyes will be viewing summer's undoing.
Her tapestries of green will disappear from the scene,
when leaves, grass and weed change to autumn tweed.

AT THIS time of the year many farmers are busy painting and fixing. You never realize how high the barn or house is until your husband is perched way up there painting the peak.

We have an anxious, uneasy feeling until they come back closer to earth. But they act so nonchalant as they try to reach these high places with a brush that they give the impression they are veteran mountain-climbers instead of men who till the soil!

THE TWO lambs that make their home on our farm are parading their fall outfits...of "barn-red" wool. With all the bright fashion colors for fall they are right in style. They picked up their colorful apparel by getting in contact with "wet paint."

Our lambs will have to wear these red stains for awhile. Soap and water will not take them off.

OUR LIVES too become stained when we aren't careful where and how we walk. But we know Someone who can cleanse every spot-

"Though your sins be as scarlet, they shall be as white as snow; though they be red like crimson, they shall be as wool." Isa. 1:18

Country Style

September 14, 1967

What are the farmers busy with in September? They never run out of work.

Many of them have been working with fence posts, woven wire and barbed wire. Fencing is a job that most farmers get at with reluctance - like we do with our patching!

Some fences needed to be mended, some replaced and some fences have been pulled out so fields will become larger.

ACCORDING TO news reports, the farmers aren't the only ones that are fencing. The barbed wire fence that will separate North and South Vietnam will be a big project...and not a friendly one! This wasn't what barbed wire was invented for.

You have maybe said bad things about "bob wire" more than once...when your clothing has caught on it, but it is one of the great "agricultural" inventions of all time.

About a century ago the westward expansion of farming was slowed by the high cost of fencing. Timber for rail fencing was scarce and expensive on the Plains. Some farmers tried planting hedgerows like those of Europe. This was a slow process, but from this prickly hedge came the idea that made the 160-acre farm homestead both possible and profitable - "barbed" wire. The purpose of the sharp barbs was to keep livestock where it belonged.

"SEPTEMBER days"
September is Mother Nature's encore to its symphony of summer. We drink in her every beauty because we know when her sunny song is over, Jack Frost will take his position on the podium.

September has all kinds of treasures. In our gardens the tomatoes are ripening on the vine. Our mum plants are in bloom. Along the roadsides clumps of goldenrod stand, their tousled yellow heads nodding in the breeze.

Now bird songs become precious for we realize they will soon be out of earshot.

Even the animals seem to enjoy September. There is no discomfort from this weather!

In the pastures the cattle contentedly rest. They have found the secret - to enjoy it while it is here! But we rush madly around, only to discover later these lovely days are gone.

THIS IS a good time to quiet our commotion-filled days and slow up to enjoy the blessings - and the One who has blessed us!

"Be still, and know that I am God."   Ps. 46:10

Country Style

September 21, 1967

Sometimes things don't turn out the way we wish they would. The custard gets watery and the lemon meringue pie weeps...and so does the silage!

At this time of the year the newspapers begin carrying numerous reports of farm accidents. As the farmer rushes around trying to get the harvest in before winter, he may not be aware of the strain his wife is under - her concern for his safety.

Danger walks beside him every day and waits for carelessness or negligence to catch him off guard. All the tasks of the fall season are done in the dangerous environment of high powered cutting machinery.

FARMERS, TAKE NOTICE!

Your loving wives have something to say -

"When you are filling the silo, we worry as you make that climb up and down the outside of a 50-60 foot silo, setting pipes for the blower. Remember you don't have wings, so go slow. Be careful and surefooted.

"For our sakes, check to see that all guards on machinery are on and in place.

"Yes, farming is a gamble, but the stakes are too high to chance risking carelessness around the cornpicker. Give up a finger, hand or life, just to save a minute or two? The cornpicker can be a ferocious flesh and bone-eating machine, so when it plugs or needs to be adjusted, please shut it off...and THEN fix it. It might take longer, but you'll be here to run it another day.

"Be wary of the deadly power take-off. It waits like a boa constrictor to seize anything that comes near and wraps it around and around - be it clothes or man.

"Above all, remember that we love you - every finger, hand and arm of you - so please, please, be extra careful this fall!"

AT THE END of day, just before dusk, a hush comes over the land. The birds twitter their evening lullabies, the cattle leisurely graze on the hills and the cows relax after being milked and fed.

The sky takes on beautiful colors as the sun begins to set.

Then I am reminded of Millet's famous old painting, "The Angelus." ...Two simple farm folks in their field at sunset, their heads bowed in prayer.

It is just as if all nature quietly folds her hands and waits for the evening benediction.

And we bow our heads too.
"The Lord bless thee, and keep thee;
The Lord make his face to shine upon
    thee and be gracious unto thee;
The Lord lift up his countenance upon
    thee and give thee peace."
Num. 6:26

Country Style

September 28, 1967

Farm bouquets.

I brought in the last glads of the season. One spike is as red as glowing embers and is named "Sans Souci." It brightens the whole room. My bouquet is in a vase on the kitchen table.

On one of my husband's trips into the corn field he picked a few of the finest ears of corn he could find there. His golden collection hangs out by the gate.

Both bouquets are beautiful!

IT NEVER fails.

I don't know about the rain in Spain, but here I've discovered that it falls mainly when the hay is down. For weeks we waited for a rain to show up and make our short alfalfa grow. The hay was finally cut anyway. Sure enough, the next day we had a lovely shower.

IT LOOKS like the cattle will have a varied diet come winter. The last cutting of hay was baled and now the silage cutter is preparing some greens for their daily menu.

When the corn is maturing and the leaves just beginning to dry, it's time to make silage.

SILO FILLING is quite an operation! This giant food chopper on wheels goes up and down the corn rows chewing the seven to nine foot stalks into shreds. Big covered silage wagons loaded with this vitamin-packed stuff begin rolling by. With all the tractors needed for this project there is plenty of noise. The green mixture is then blown up into the silo. But you will notice there is something missing - the familiar silage fragrance! That comes with aging.

THE SWALLOWS like to line up on the electric wires outside the barn. There they sit in a row, dressed in their swallow-tailed coats. They remind me of people in their Sunday-best, sitting in a pew attentively listening to the preacher.

And they know secrets that we will never understand. Soon God's radar will guide them to a comfortable winter home. And they are trusting enough to follow His leading.

Are we?

"I will instruct you and teach you the way you should go; I will counsel you with my eye upon you."

Ps. 32:8

Country Style

October 5, 1967

This summer we didn't even notice the plain old vine growing on the fence...but now its leaves have turned to shades of deep red and burgundy and its beauty demands our attention.

It's a delight to find beauty in unexpected places.

Now is the time to feast our eyes on the rich colors of the trees as they daily change from greens to golds and browns. This profusion of beauty is the swan song of the leaves before their days are ended.

IT'S FUNNY how accustomed we had become to the tall green cornfields and now how bare the sections that were cut for silage look. These empty spaces are just as noticeable as the gap where the missing tooth used to be.

THE SOYBEAN fields have certainly changed their looks. It is hard to believe they are the same as the green, full of foliage fields that were walked through last summer.

Now all the leaves have fallen off and the straight little stalks stand holding onto their bean pods. When the combine goes through, the farmer will get paid in beans for all the work he has had with them.

JACK FROST has been here. One night he tiptoed around so lightly and quietly that we weren't even aware that he had paid us a call until later when some of the cornfields took a pale sickly look.

But on his next visit his frosty footprints could still be seen early the next morning on the grass and the cars.

It's hard to think kindly of him for there is nothing lovely about his killing touch to flowers, trees and grass.

THE FARMER'S voice shatters the dark early morning stillness with his familiar "C'm boss!" This sound is like a bugle call to the milk cows and they move into line and head for the barn door.

They soon know which stall is theirs and march directly into it, where a helping of ground feed is waiting for them. With the choice of stalls there could be mass confusion if a cow or two should decide to try another one. (And they sometimes do!)

Cows are really quite intelligent, for only the group that will be milked at the first shift comes at the first call. The rest remain "at ease" until it is their turn.

The cows know their own stall. They also know their master's voice and when he calls "C'm boss!" they usually obey.

AND SOMETIMES livestock are smarter than people.

"The ox knoweth his owner, and the ass his master's crib, but My people do not know!" (Isa. 1:3)

Country Style

October 12, 1967

The October wind makes a
rustling sound.
As cornstalks shuffle
And leaves come tumbling down.

THIS IS football weather. Where you find several boys together, you'll most likely discover a football game in progress. This brisk air is perfect for sports.

From my kitchen window I can watch the antics of the little calves. This weather seems to make them sports-minded too. They have their own version of football.

They all rush off in one direction, running after each other, their tails wildly waving behind them. It looks like someone heading for a touchdown with the rest in pursuit.

FOXES HAVE always had a liking for chickens. And foxes, coons and skunks still hang around henhouses and try to carry off chickens.

Raising chickens gets to be a 24 hour-a-day job when you are awakened at 2 a.m. to shoot four-legged prowlers.

People who raise chickens don't need any more problems. With only 20 cents a dozen for eggs and 4 cents a pound for old hens, things are bad enough to make them sit down and cry.

COMBINES ARE very fussy machines. The early morning hours are not for them. It often is almost noon before soybean pods are not too tough to shell, and they start rolling.

This isn't because they are lazy or have union hours, but because dampness makes the job impossible. They have to wait for some sunshine to dry the field out.

YOU CAN do wonders with WEEDS!

They really can be made into lovely wintertime arrangements. Now is the time to pick grasses, weeds and milkweed pods. A can of spray paint will give them some color and they will bring enjoyment when fresh flowers are gone.

HOW HELPLESS we are when the electricity is off!

The REA was doing some work out here and our current had to be off for several hours. Everything in the house came to a standstill that morning.

The clock stopped, the clothes were half-washed. I couldn't even get the dishes done because the water pump wouldn't run.

It made me realize how dependent I am on the power in those wires. There is very little I can do without it.

AND IT REMINDED ME of the greater power available to me...and I am even more helpless without Him!

"Apart from Me ye can do nothing!" John 15:5

Country Style

October 19, 1967

Trees are contrary things!

While we have been getting out our sweaters and jackets and bundling up to keep warm, the trees have been undressing.

They toss their coats of leaves at their feet and face the winter bare-limbed.

OCTOBER seems rather late in the season for picnicking, but when the corn silage cutting jobs are finished, our neighbor puts on a steak fry for families he did custom filling for.

Cities may have their office parties, but farm people who have worked side by side have their get-togethers too, country-style. The men talk machinery and crops, the women visit and the children usually are busy with a ball of some kind. And we all eat!

When you're dressed warm and these good tender steaks are hot and sizzling, it gets to be the best picnic of the year!

THIS IS National Apple Week.

Our apple tree was a disappointment this year and had nothing to present us but leaves. But we can still celebrate National Apple Week.

We don't have to be reminded to use apples. In fact, who can resist the displays of these red gems in the stores? We are drawn to them just as Eve was.

Apples can be twice enjoyed. These polished red beauties are a delight to the eye and also a treat to eat. Now apples are at their best, crisp and tasty, and plentiful.

With all the variety of ways to prepare them, we can almost serve them three times a day and not tire of them. And to top it off, they're good for us!

And breathes there a man who doesn't love apple pie?

THE HONKING of wild geese was the first sound that greeted me one dark early morning. These birds must have been flying all night and now they swooped low over our house and gave us the full benefit of their noisy honking chorus. They were off on their journey to a warmer climate.

I heard the howling wind and thought, "What a day for an air trip!" But they sounded confident and excited as they sailed into a new day and turned their cries heavenward and out of my hearing.

THEN I WAS REMINDED that I, too, had a day's journey ahead of me...24 new hours to live and work in. I wondered if my day's journey would be blustery and frustrating or a sunny and pleasant one. And I too turned my voice heavenward-

"How precious to me are Thy thoughts, O God,
How vast is the sum of them.
When I awake, I am still with Thee." Ps. 139:17, 18.

Country Style

October 26, 1967

At a glance, the cornfields look like wasteland, desolate and unkempt. The brittle stalks have been breaking and the dry leaves blowing off.

But through the farmer's eyes these fields still have beauty for he knows there is treasure hiding there. Beneath those dry husks hang ears of gold. Its forlorn appearance doesn't fool him. And he intends to do something about it!

He must get ready for this new treasure. You will find the farmer shelling his old corn so he can make room for the new. And it's time to get the corn picker out!

The farmer hopes there is enough treasure in those fields to pay expenses and leave him a little for all his work. But he's afraid that this year the nuggets may be rather dainty and diminutive.

The Farmer's Dilemma
I have an uncomfortable feeling
That I can't seem to shrug...
The cost - price squeeze has now become
More of a wrestler's bear hug!

LITTLE PIGS get into mischief too!

Children go through a certain stage when they manage to get into everything. We have some little 25-lb pigs that give us the same trouble.

They are small enough to squeeze through the tiniest opening and you will see them always on the run...here, there and everywhere... getting their little noses into everything.

I think they know they are doing wrong for when they see or hear us, they scamper off at full speed. I suppose they are having just as much fun as a little girl in her mother's cosmetic drawer or a little boy who has found a mud puddle.

There is one consolation. Soon they'll get too big to squeeze through these holes!

EVERY TIME I go out the door, Pepper seems to be waiting with a hungry look in her eyes... hungry for food and attention. She can't speak, but I get the message and retrace my steps to find her a choice morsel, plus a few kind words and a pat.

When she gives me that trusting look, I just can't disappoint her.

AND THERE is One the whole world looks to...
"The eyes of all look to thee, O Lord;
Thou givest them their food in due season
Thou openest thy hand, and satisfieth the desire of every living thing."   Ps. 145:15,16

Country Style

November 2, 1967

Time Marches On!
I've been known as "daughter", "cousin" and "sis";
Then "wife" when I changed to Mrs. from Miss.
Next I received some new attention...
Being called "Mom" gave added dimension
Now I have reached a still higher plateau-
I became "Grandma" a week ago!

SEVERAL TIMES a day there is a lot of congestion at the pasture gate. At times it seems to be just as much of a traffic snarl as we find at rush hour on a busy intersection.

When the whole herd of cows decides to go to pasture at once and there is only room for two animals to go through the gate, a bottleneck develops.

Occasionally one cow decides to stop at the gate and leisurely watch the traffic on the highway, holding up the entire procession. But cows don't get irritated, rev their motors or lay on the horn. They just patiently wait for her to make up her mind.

It doesn't matter to them whether they arrive where they are going in five minutes or an hour.

SOMETIMES THE farmer's wife gets tired of her farm chores... washing the milking machine, packing eggs and always fixing meals and lunches for extra men.

But then one day her husband comes home from the field with a beautiful colored ear of corn he has found or a bouquet of wild flowers and presents them to her...and she feels richer than the highest paid career women in town!

OUR YARD LIGHT is burned out and it's amazing how long the path between the car and the kitchen door seems in the darkness. Now we must slowly find our way, hoping we won't trip over something and sprain an ankle. It is even hard to stay on the sidewalk.

When we get a new light bulb inserted we will again be able to walk in safety and confidence.

HOW UNCERTAIN we are of our path when we walk in darkness! But we needn't stumble and fumble...

"I am the light of the world; he who follows me will not walk in darkness, but will have the light of life." John 8:12

Country Style

November 9, 1967

The farmer hates to see leftovers go to waste! At this time of the year he's liable to lay in a new supply of feeder cattle so he can make use of the corn ears and roughage left in the field.

In the fall there usually are plenty of feeders looking for homes. Calves have been coming in from the western ranges and now many farmers are listening to these homesick feeder calves bawl.

As we drive along the highway it is interesting to take note of the shopping each farmer has been doing. In some fields we see pretty black Angus calves; some farmers have a liking for neat Herefords and some prefer husky-looking Shorthorns.

And from the looks of some of the calves you would think these farmers were going into the dairy business. (Often these calves are more of the Twiggy type.)

The farmer has to look at these faces for a while so he prefers to buy the fancier grades. It is nicer to come out every day to a yard full of Angus, Herefords, or Shorthorns... rather than each morning to face a collection of this and that. But if the price is right, he can stand it!

"**CALL THE** rendering truck!"
When the farmer's wife hears these instructions, she thinks "there goes the profits!"

In every occupation you expect some losses and set-backs, but when she sees this truck drive away she can't help but reflect on "what might have been" if that animal could have been marketed. It could have bought a new dress...or that something she has been wanting for the house.

She is happiest when the rendering truck's stops are few and far between.

THE OTHER day I saw three sparrows splashing in a puddle. It was rather late in the season for outdoor bathing, but they seemed to be having a wonderful time.

With the lack of puddles this summer and fall, they probably were overjoyed at the luxury of a bath, even though it was a bit chilly.

Then I was reminded that I wasn't the only one watching these drab little birds..and it was very comforting to remember...

"For His eye is on the sparrow...
And I know He cares for me!"

Country Style

November 16, 1967

It's corn-picking time!
The littered-looking farm yards indicate it...and the weary-looking farmers show it.
These days the farmer is driven by a compulsion to get his corn picked before a snow comes. He fears a heavy snow that will force him to leave some of his corn in the field.

WE ALL seem to have more than our share of corn husks this year. The fall breeze gets a hold of these and they come sailing onto the lawn and everywhere. Only on a damp morning does this litter get left in the field.
This fall many corn ears seem to come "with their wrappers on." They go into the cribs individually wrapped...just as neatly as peaches in a crate. It's hard to see the golden corn color in the bins because of the husk.

THE WATER fountain is a popular gathering place for the feeder calves.
After an exploring expedition into the cornfield they head for the fountain and wait their turn. They are like a gang of children just in from play who line up for their drink of water.

November Query
Lonely leaf on the tree,
Aren't you tired of clinging?
Your holding on
Won't prevent
Winter from springing.

THE SHARP cool wind lets us know that fall is slipping away and winter will soon be moving in for his annual sojourn.
The farmer has been gradually bundling up a little more every day. He has gotten out his hooded sweatshirts and parkas.
He isn't as lucky as our sheep who arrive at the chilly season with their woolies on.
The farmer has put the comfort cover on his tractor and he really appreciates the protection this gives. Corn-picking can be the coldest job he has all year.

I THINK almost every farmer has been pleasantly surprised as he started unloading his corn and figured his bushels per acre.
He just stands there and shakes his head in unbelief, wondering how he could get this much corn from the little rainfall we had.
It is one of those things that he must credit to his miracle-working Partner.
"Call unto me and I will answer thee and show thee great and mighty things which thou knowest not." Jer. 33:3

Country Style

November 23, 1967

What is this "stuff" called thankfulness?

Thankfulness is being grateful for the warm, cozy feeling that comes when everyone is home at night, safe. Thankfulness is appreciating a blanket, and a bed to put it on. Thankfulness is joy for a hurt that doesn't hurt any more, or for knowing how to live with a hurt that still hurts.

Thankfulness is looking at your peaceful acres and being relieved that they are not war-torn. Thankfulness is that feeling you have when your complete family is seated around the table, their heads bowed in prayer, and there is plenty of good food to satisfy all.

Fall asks an attitude of thanksgiving. For each kernel the farmer now has many ears of corn, for each cow he now has a calf dividend, and for each smile and act of kindness he has a friend.

AND WHEN we're counting our blessings, let's not forget one of the best - "friends"! They are the golden threads that God weaves into the tapestry of our lives. They are placed along life's pathway so we have someone not only to share our times of joy and sorrow, but a friend is what the heart needs all the time.

THESE DAYS my thoughts are with a special friend...and the many others who are feeling the pangs of bereavement.

To a Friend in Sorrow

Dear friend...
My heart too aches because you grieve.
Each thought begets a prayer for you.
And though we may be miles apart,
I weep today...with you.

FROM MY kitchen window I can watch the fall activity. In the distance a bright red wagon travels up and down the corn rows, the corn picker spout hanging over it irregularly burping out ears of corn.

Outside our puppies scamper and tumble. They resemble little teddy bears, plump and furry. Any little bit of attention or food sets their little tails in motion.

I guess they get so full of gratitude on the inside that it starts their tails a-wagging.

AT THIS time of the year, our hearts too should almost burst with gratitude...with the result that we cannot contain it but must give it expression by word and action -

"What shall I render to the Lord for all his bounty to me?" Ps. 116:12

Country Style

November 30, 1967

Usually our milk cows are a prim and sedate bunch...but on the first day into the freshly-harvested cornfield, they are as excited as if they had embarked on a trip to Europe.

They waste no time taking it all in. When they discover they are in new territory, they kick up their heels and take a sightseeing tour into every corner of the field.

It looks like part of the fun is finding the tasty tidbits hiding here and there. I suppose someone who does some hunting or fishing would understand this. There is enjoyment in eating the catch - but the greater part of the fun is in the hunting.

THE FARMER can now get at all the things he was going to do "when I get through picking corn!" It really got to be quite a list.

And he had better not forget those jobs he promised to help his wife with!

The corn picker has been parked in the shed for another year and the farmer was thankful it lasted through another season. He hopes things will look up by next fall so maybe he can invest in a new one, but with the $4,000 price tag on it, he wonders.

In the past, the investment of a dollar husking hook was all that was needed to harvest his corn. The farmer would get out his faithful team of horses and the lumber wagon with its high bang boards and walk up and down the corn rows, unsituating the ears, one by one, from their moorings.

The team learned to move at the speed of the human picker. They would mosey along as he ripped off the husk and tossed the ear into the bang-board.

The only casualties in those days were a sprained wrist and a stiff back.

In comparing then and now, we wonder if there isn't a price to pay for progress, both money-wise and accident-wise.

NOW THE farmer has brought the harvest in...to barn, to granary, to bin.

The alfalfa that covered acres of land now is stacked in the hayloft. The corn that stood mile on mile is piled in cribs.

Our corncrib looks like a bright red cornucopia, with the corn ears spilling out from its alley.

The farmer has squeezed his whole farm into hayloft, silo and cribs.

"The earth has yielded its
   increase.
God, our God, has blessed us."
                               Ps. 67:6

Country Style

December 7, 1967

December has arrived with her sullen disposition. Sometimes her skies look as dark and foreboding as a child's face just before he bursts into tears. And December's gray countenance usually is a forecast of moisture in some form too.

But even if her days are short or the weather dreary, young and old have excitement in their hearts, for this is the happy month of Christmas.

COUNTRY LIVING has a tempo of its own. During the busy seasons of spring, summer and fall, the farmer feels like he has been working to the hectic accompaniment of Leroy Anderson's "Typewriter Song." Life has been "work, work, work" - with no let down!

Now that the harvest is in, he can catch his breath and life can slow down to more of a waltz time. Now the farmer can afford to linger over his morning coffee, or settle down in his favorite chair after the noon meal and really take time to read the paper. The chores don't need to be a grand rush now and he has time for some country "living."

THESE DAYS the pigs are having a little variety in their menu. Besides the regular ground feed, they are eating corn on the cob. When this is scooped into the pigyard every day, you should see how busy they get! It compares to a crowd of women digging at a bargain table.

The pigs poke their noses here and there amongst the husks, trying to find some "snootworn" merchandise that they can get their teeth into. Now the self feeder full of ground feed doesn't interest them. They keep rummaging through these husks long after everything eatable is gone.

IF YOU glance in the direction of the feed yards you are liable to discover the farmer leaning on the fence, watching his cattle. This is one of his favorite pastimes now. If the cattle are doing well, you may notice a gleam of pride in his eyes. Here while he watches them eat, he does some of his planning and dreaming.

He studies his cattle and is quick to notice an animal that isn't feeling up to par. His eyes move from one head to another as he sizes up each animal's progress.

AND SOMEONE has His eyes on us too...

"For the eyes of the Lord run to and fro throughout the whole earth, to show his might in behalf of those whose heart is perfect toward him." 2 Chron. 16:9

Country Style

December 14, 1967

In these days before Christmas everyone is in a rush. We discover short tempers and ill humors. This is the time to use "grace notes" in our daily living.

Grace notes are those small trills that the composer puts into a piece of music to add charm and beauty to it.

And we can put grace notes in our life...by a twinkle in our eye, a bit of humor, warmth in our greeting and going out of our way for others. They are the personal touch, the little extras that bring delight to others and add beauty and charm to our own lives.

I GUESS growing up can be a painful process for animals too.

The stock cows "spoil" their offspring by letting them tag along with mother until they are almost half-grown. When the time comes for them to be cut loose from mother's apron strings, the calves really throw some noisy tantrums.

When the farmer happens to have 50 or 60 of these crybabies fussing at once, he can't keep their behavior a secret. In calf language they are hollering, "I want my mama!" A-nyone who drives onto the farmyard is greeted by this sound.

After a few nights of this disturbing racket, the children in the family plead to sleep in a bedroom that doesn't face the cattleyards.

CHRISTMAS BAKING is full of traditions and memories. Each year we make old favorites that Grandma got us accustomed to...like krandser, sandbakkelse and spritz. And they are all hard on the butter supply.

Just think, in Grandma's day she first had to churn all the butter she used in her recipes. And I complain that Christmas baking is a lot of work today!

YOU MUST read the article "In Praise of Pigs" in the December Reader's Digest. It will give you more than one chuckle. I guess we just haven't been looking at the pig from an appreciative point of view.

The fact that a pig's heart closely resembles a human heart is very interesting. The mechanisms of both hearts are similar...but I hate to admit there are other heart similarities too, and these are not in praise of pigs...or man!

For instance, pigs are known for their selfishness. They aren't a bit concerned about the welfare of the other pigs...only that they get plenty for themselves.

And pigs have a craving for wallowing in the mud and find enjoyment in getting all dirtied.

I think all of us have discovered these distasteful inclinations deep in our own hearts...even if they only show up in our thoughts.

PIGS WILL be pigs. But people don't have to be!

"Create in me a clean heart, O God, and put a new and right spirit within me." Ps. 51:10

Country Style

December 21, 1967

Some things haven't changed too much in 1,900 years. We can still see flocks of sheep grazing on the hillsides. Shepherds have been replaced by fences, but sheep still need someone to look after them and see that they are in a safe place at night.

Today there is not much danger from wild animals, but many a sheep has been lost when strange dogs get to frolicking among them.

Our woolly trio has to mingle with the cows. They tag along to the cornfield and are part of the procession when they come back to the barnyard. While the cows are being milked they sneak over to the feed bunks and lunch on the cow's silage. They seem to hold their own in this predominately bovine community.

BABIES AND Christmas go together.

No gift is greater prized at Christmas time...or on any day...than a baby's smile. Especially if it's a new granddaughter's!

Like a rose it unfolds. The sweet rosebud mouth quickly opens to full flower, giving us heavenly delight.

This little spontaneous act can melt your heart and make you respond by feeling deeply love-indebted to this precious bundle of angel sweetness.

Oh, farmer folk,
Let your heart sing out,
For you know what Christmas
Is all about.

'Twas to farmer folk keeping watch by night
That angels came in glory bright.

You've seen a manger,
and tended sheep:
You know the quietness
when animals sleep.

It was in a barn
where livestock stayed,
where cobwebs hung
and donkeys brayed:
There in a dim and dusty stall
Was born the Lord and King of all!

Oh, farmer folk,
Let your voice ring out;
Tell the world what
Christmas is all about!

"JOY TO THE WORLD, THE LORD IS COME!"

Country Style

December 28, 1967

Before Christmas everyone was busy "*decorating*"...Christmas trees, cookies and packages.

Mother Nature decided to try her hand at it too and she really went overboard. She went to work on the trees and glazed each twig and every branch. She made intricate designs out of weeds and grasses. The iced woven wire fences were done in ornamental filigree.

Looking out on this decorated world, it reminded me of a beautifully decorated wedding cake - with dreamy peaks and showy artistry.

But she was careless when doing her decorating and the spilled icing underfoot wasn't appreciated by anyone.

There was more than one dairyman who would gladly have traded this winter wonderland for a day in May as he sat alongside the cows, milking "by hand" because the electricity was off. When you aren't in practice those arm muscles tire in a hurry!

EVERY FAMILY observes Christmas in a different way. Some have their activities on Christmas Eve; others wait until Christmas day.

Some families always have lutefisk and lefse; others enjoy oyster stew or plum pudding. These traditions weave past and present into one happy tune.

IF YOU considered ham for Christmas dinner, you probably got to wondering what happened to the pig after you sold it at 18 cents a pound. that could make ham worth more than 90 cents a pound.

Was the pig sent on a expensive excursion around the world...or did Midas touch it and make it pure gold?

Christmas is - greetings...and hospitality...and family,,,and excitement. But through it all we are aware of its true meaning and each year the blessed story grows more dear to us.

IN A STABLE

Oh, lowly barn,
Tonight you softly beckon me
To pause in your abode.

No decorated palace this...
No dainty nursery here.

I probe the Christmas mysteries:
My voice breaks through the
    dusk...
"Why would He leave a heavenly
    throne
To come to earth for this?"

Then a soft sound answers me,
A pigeon's kindly coo.
It so clearly enunciates...
"For you! For you!"
And cows and kittens join the
    song...
"For you! For you!"   II Cor. 8:9

Country Style

January 4, 1968

Many little farm boys are busy playing with miniature equipment that they found under the Christmas tree. Diminutive tractors, plows, disks, corn pickers, wagons...and almost any item that the real farmer has.

If you will look out the window you will discover that these are the same color and make as Dad's!

The farmer takes pride in the make of equipment he uses. He'll argue long and strong on its merits. If he is a green machinery man you won't catch him with a piece of red equipment...and vice versa.

Even when it comes to buying toys for his children he'll stick with his favorite brand.

And a tractor and plow "just like Dad's" makes it 100 percent more wonderful.

AT THIS time of the year our Shetland pony is just plain homely.

During the summer her coat was sleek and a rich brown color. Then she held her head high and was full of zip. When winter arrived, her coat became dull and shaggy and mottled and gray.

I think even she is aware of the shabby impression she makes because now she stands by herself, with a sad expression and a lowered head. She looks about as dilapidated as Old Father Time.

Her long straggly mane and disheveled appearance give her kind of a hippie look.

THE DAYS of 1967 are now memories...both glad and sad.

New calendars are hanging on our walls This year a rose calendar we received from a friend adorns our kitchen. Each month will show us a painting of a lovely rose with an accompanying quotation.

I would like to share this Irish Blessing as my wish for your new year...

"Sure, and may there be a road before you and it bordered with roses, the likes of which have ne'er been smelt or seen before, for their warm fine color and the great sweetness that is on them."

MAY YOUR 1968 journey be a pleasant one.

And to get on this scenic rose-bordered route, stay on Psalms 37:4 for the next 365 days...

"Delight thyself also in the Lord and He will give thee the desires of thine heart."

Country Style

January 11, 1968

"To slop the pigs, or not to slop the pigs" - that is the question. And the verdict will probably remain just as unresolved as the answer to whether or not you should dunk your doughnut.

With the coming of self-feeders and ground feed, the old swill barrel went out of date. But now the merits of this liquid feed are again being weighed. And equipment is being made so it can be done automatically.

Way back in the dim past many of us can remember the big barrel that stood by the hog house. Here the skim milk was dumped after every milking, some corn or oats added and it was set to soak.

The pigs must have thought it was a delicious concoction, for they would almost knock the farmer down as he delivered it to their long troughs.

IN JANUARY, Mother Nature is apt to turn the thermostat down to below zero temperatures. But this doesn't give the farmer an excuse to sit in by the fire. He has to take a chance on being nipped by Jack Frost and get out to do the chores.

It's hard for him to decide which is worse..."doing" the chores in cold weather, or "dreading" to go out and do them.

THIS COLD weather brings problems with it. The water fountains freeze up! The tractor won't start! And who wants to struggle with these things when the cold wind blows through your wraps and you can see your breath?

The animals look like they have had their noses in the flour bin, and even the farmer gets frosty after several hours of chores.

On these cold days, our Ferdinand resembles a dragon breathing fire and smoke as he stands and bellows, each bellow sending forth puffs of white frosty breath.

EVEN WHEN the weather is cold, Pepper likes to be outside so she can come and go as she pleases, and so she can keep watch on things.

"Twenty below" weather or not, she feels she has to be out by the gate to see us off and welcome us home. We can tell she is uncomfortable as she holds up one foot off the frozen ground, and then the other.

When she has performed her duty, she runs to her place of refuge, a niche in the pile of bales where the north wind cannot reach her, and where, when the sun is out, she is in a position to catch every winter sunbeam.

SOMETIMES cold winds of adversity blow around us, and the frigid fingers of discouragement want to get a grip on us, then we too can run to our place of refuge and be warmed in the sunshine of his love.

"Thou art my hiding place."
Ps. 119:114

Country Style

January 18, 1968

The people who think the days of exciting living are over, haven't heard farmers tell of their perils when the bull goes on the rampage.

Almost every farmer has had a few moments of dangerous living that he can tell about. And according to the details on the front page of the newspapers, some farmers don't live to tell about theirs.

The pioneers' experiences with the Indians weren't a bit more dangerous than when a pawing, snorting bull is headed your way. There isn't one of these animals that can be trusted. In their fury, they have even been known to bust their way out of a truck.

When an angry one encircles your house, you wish you had a few guns to poke through the windows to ward him off TV style. It's for sure, words are of no use at a time like this.

Most farmers who notice their animal becoming bad tempered think it is wiser to make hamburger out of him than to give him a second chance.

"How good the outdoors makes the indoors feel!" It all depends on how you look at things.

SOMETIMES we're so busy complaining about winter that we miss the little quiet joys, the "winter joys" that can give that warm happy feeling.

What might some of these be? A valentine morning, when the world is frosty and lacy; the sparkling whiteness of the snow when the sun shines on it; the security and shelter of home on a stormy night; round snow-topped corncribs that resemble frosted cupcakes; tracks in the new fallen snow.

And how about...fresh doughnuts, the aroma of baking bread, a good book on a wintry evening, a game of checkers...and popcorn? None of these give as much enjoyment in the heat of summer.

A drab world turned to white reminds us to turn our hearts upward and pray for holiness.

"Wash me, and I shall be whiter than snow." Ps. 51:7

Here We Go Again!
Mr. Farmer, I've some news to break,
(Better take it sitting down.)
A 5 to 7 percent machinery price hike
Is rumored coming 'round.

Country Style

January 25, 1968

With winter's late sunrises, we can all tune in morning's arrival. And it comes in color! Rosy and lavender shades line the eastern horizon. As we watch, the colors gradually rise, tint the clouds, and then fade away into daylight.

I had to smile when I discovered that high in the western sky the moon was still shining, and it too seemed to be taking in God's "Today" show.

THIS MONTH the farm family's spare time isn't spent in family games like Scrabble or Monopoly. Now they are busy with the complicated game of Income Tax. And Uncle Sam always seems to end up as the winner!

With all the checks to sort and columns to add, it gets to be a family affair.

Farming doesn't only involve tractors, plows and corn-pickers. At this time of the year, the farmer's equipment includes paper, pencil, canceled checks and bank statements. Now he's a white-collared worker in overalls.

When he adds the columns and columns of expenses (gas, fertilizer, seed, feed, etc.) and these get into the four and five figure numbers, he begins to wonder if he really can afford to farm.

Bills, bills, bills! The only time you can get any pleasure from them is when you can use them as tax exemptions.

THERE ARE times when the farmer's wife doesn't have to ask the farmer what he has been doing. When he comes in from cleaning the hog house, or has been up in the silo, the tell-tale odor speaks for itself.

These new soaps were made for times like these.

WHENEVER the farmer goes into the barnyard, two sheep come running. They trot along behind him as he does his chores there.

These overgrown bottle-lambs haven't outgrown their attachment for him. Although he no longer gives them a bottle, they know that he still will lead them to good eating places, where they can snack as he shovels out silage or pitches hay. They have learned that if they follow him, they will be provided for.

When they tag along with him, they are really living!

AND TAGGING along with the Good Shepherd is even better! "The Lord is my shepherd; I shall not want." Ps. 23:1

Country Style

February 1, 1968

Marches, overtures and rhapsodies.

The spirited and uplifting music of the band is just the tonic we need at this time of the year. We come away from a band concert with a new appreciation and awareness of sounds.

If we keep our ears open, we discover that the farm presents a daily rhapsody. When we hear the crescendos of the wind soughing through the trees, we can almost imagine the woodwinds playing. The birds twitter in flute like sounds. The clanging of the hog self-feeders give emphasis like the cymbal.

And along comes the penetrating squeal of a pig in oboe-tones.

The precise click of the electric water pump gives the definite beat of the snare drum, and the deep-toned tuba is represented by the cow's "moo."

During the winter, the arrangements we hear are more on the quiet side, until the little calves come in with their beginner's brass choir, or the tractor plays its trombone-like solo.

The farm symphony of sounds usually doesn't have a very tuneful repertoire, and often gives the impression of an orchestra warming up.

TODAY, laying in a meat supply isn't a seasonal job. Now a steer or hog can be butchered any time of the year.

But in the days before freezers and lockers, this was the time of the year that the farmer did his own butchering. Then the weather was cold enough so some meat could be kept frozen in the shanty or on the back porch.

Butchering was a big project. Usually the farmer's wife would process quarts and quarts of meatballs and roast beef, and render her year's supply of lard. The meat to be used for hamburger had to be ground with a hand grinder.

Both delicacies and commonplace staples were prepared. Who of the older folks can't remember "speke kjott" (dried beef), which was often stored in the oats bin...and the old standby, salt pork?

Every eatable part of the animal was used. Head cheese was made from the head; suet was utilized for mincemeat and homemade soap. Often the blood was used in some way. Even the bones were taken care of, for at butchering time the dogs had a feast and were busy digging their surplus away for future enjoyment.

THE FARMER gets his exercise even during the winter months. If he is a dairyman, he does his calisthenics faithfully every morning and evening as he lifts and empties the milk buckets.

He does bending exercises as he loads and unloads the bales of hay and straw that are needed to keep his livestock full and clean. These all help to keep him trim.

EXERCISE keeps our bodies healthy...but there is more to keeping in shape-

"For bodily exercise profiteth little; but godliness is profitable unto all things, having promise of the life that now is, and of that which is to come." I Tim. 4:8

Country Style

February 8, 1968

"O wind, if winter comes, can spring be far behind?"

Winter's days are numbered. How do I know? Spring styles have appeared in store windows and I discovered thoughts of spring in a farmer's heart.

During these pre-spring days the farmer optimistically looks forward to a new and better year as he plans and prepares for another cycle of sowing and reaping. He is being given another chance to find out what his fertile acres can do.

It has always been this way. This was the time of the year when Grandfather was the jolliest and happiest...when his mind was full of plans for another year and before spring and summer's burden of too much work and too little rain took the enthusiasm out of his step.

About this time of the year he made many trips to the granary, checking the choice ears of corn hanging overhead in the alley. These were the days before hybrid seed corn when each farmer had to grow his own seed corn. The best ears were sorted out at corn-picking time and then hung up to dry. His next year's corn crop depended on them.

After he shelled this corn, he planted some kernels in a can of soil to get a preview of its germination. And always his dream for a new growing season was "This one will be the best!"

THE BAD penny always returns! My "bad penny" has four legs, a missing tail and a bad temperament...and she's back again!

Last summer a crabby old cat decided to make her place of residence on our back doorstep. Somewhere she had lost her tail...and maybe a psychiatrist would ascribe her bad temperament to this tragedy in her past.

Then several months ago she disappeared, and her absence at the back door didn't make me sad. But it didn't last. Now she's back again, with her same grabby manners and crabby "meows".

How can you convince a cat that she isn't welcome?

JUST A "has been"!

No footprints in the snow. No smoke from the chimney. Quietness all around.

The windows are boarded up and the buildings are in need of paint. Brush is growing around the door. In the background, a rickety windmill stands.

We feel a touch of sadness as we pass neglected homesteads that have been left people-less. But they haven't always been so. Once they were home, with flowers growing by the back door, windows that sparkled, and where voices of children could be heard. There was a time when the windmill stood straight and responded to every whim of the wind.

Each farmstead, if it could speak, would have an interesting story to tell. These rooms could tell of happy days...a bride and groom, a baby's gurgles, a mother singing at her work, the sound of prayers as a family gathered for evening devotions.

(continued)

(February 8, 1968 – continued)

Each empty house also has its sad memories to reveal...of sickness, death, bitterness, bad crops, reverses. When they boarded up the windows and doors, they shut in many lifetimes of memories, both joyous and sorrowful.

The years have had their decaying effect on these buildings and now their usefulness seems to be over.

They are just "has beens"!

IN THIS world of change and decay, nothing is lasting. But we can look forward to what will be...

"For here we have no continuing city, but we seek one to come." Heb. 13:14

Country Style

February 15, 1968

The farmer will be spending some "nights out" now. But his wife doesn't worry too much for he isn't far away. A lot of his time will be spent in the hoghouse as his new pig crop makes its appearance.

He feels it's wisest to be there and see that these newcomers get a good start in the world. The little ones he saves may mean the difference between profit and loss.

THEY SAY mealtime should be a peaceful and happy time. But, poor Pepper! With the Cat waiting to grab her lunch, she now has to eat her meals with a growl in her throat.

I wouldn't be surprised if she ends up with indigestion.

IT'S GOOD to see something green again. A flatbed loaded with bales is setting outside. The color of the hay is just as fresh and green as when it was baled.

Now our world is a charcoal drawing, but our eyes are getting anxious for it to turn green again.

MISERY is having to tell your husband not to buy you a valentine box of candy because you can't stand the calories!

Valentine's Day has come and gone, but I hope glimmers of love linger on.

A POEM I came across reminded me of our tendency to be tight-lipped and reserved when it comes to expressing our love to our dear ones. It's a rather sad tale, entitled "We Never Had Time", and it hit home!

Life can get so busy with farming and family that we never take time for each other.

"Sometimes she would look at him sitting there
Hunched and tired in the rocking chair
And long to lay a hand on his shoulder
Or smooth his hair; but when you get older
Such things seem silly. It is sort of as though
Loving was something you ought not to show.
So she never did, and he never knew
The many times she hankered to.
Now he is gone and she lives with regrets.
It isn't just death make a body sad.
It's not to have done what you wish you had."

And Valentine's Day usually gives us a nudge in the right direction.

THERE ARE all kinds of valentines - comic, big, little, old-fashioned and beautiful. You can get one with the right message for everyone, baby, sweetheart, Mother or husband.

There are heavenly valentines too...sent straight from a Father's heart. One of them says...

"How do I love thee?"
Then He showed me His son at Calvary.   John 3:16

Country Style

February 22, 1968

Some of our calves lost their wild west appearance the other day when the veterinarian paid us a visit and removed horns of assorted sizes.

After listening to the bawling and noise coming from beyond the barn, I came to the conclusion that this ordeal must be much worse than tooth extractions.

The commotion attracted our curious cows, who had to investigate as usual. But it wasn't long before they all ran off in the opposite direction. It probably dawned on them that they might be next if they stayed around.

Whether it is extracting teeth or horns, we'll have to admit that these aren't the pleasantest of happenings. But the calves had one advantage; they didn't have to go through the dreading period that we have while waiting for our appointment. And I've discovered that this needless dreading often turns out to be more painful than the actual dental work.

THE SUBJECT of garbage has been in the news lately. The farmer is quick to sympathize with the big city's problem for he knows how quickly refuse accumulates. It doesn't take long for the pile behind the barn to turn into mountainous proportions.

And he knows it doesn't disappear by magic, but takes many tedious trips back and forth to the fields. It is a year-round job that he never seems to get caught up on.

EVERY WEEK the farmer is getting invitations to eat out. There are pancake feeds and free noon meals. It seems that the fertilizer and weed spray companies have picked up the adage "The way to a man's heart is through his stomach" and changed it to further their ends.

Food always is a drawing card, but, really, the farmer receives more than food at these get-togethers. He needs to know all the latest facts concerning these chemicals and how and when to use them.

IT'S FUN to watch the little calves eating hay. They have their own lunch counter, with sort of a help-yourself arrangement. When they're hungry, all they have to do is stick their heads in the opening, grab a mouthful and chew away to their heart's content.

THE CALVES have their hay, and the farmer his pancakes, but you can't feed a soul on pancakes, corn, hay, bonds or greenbacks. Yet there is delicious and nutritious food available for it...

"How sweet are Thy words unto my taste!

Yea, sweeter than honey to my mouth!" Psalms 119:103

Country Style

February 29, 1968

March first is farm moving time. Some years we are reluctant to see it come because a special neighbor is leaving.

Years of neighboring can form strong ties. The cups of coffee we've enjoyed together. The work we've done side by side. The concerns and joys we've shared. It will be a while before we get used to not having them there.

But what if the path to their home will be a little longer now? Moving to another home doesn't mean they are moving out of our lives.

FEEL ALL out of kilter? Nothing seems to suit?

At this time of the year, we need something to pep up our sluggish dispositions. But instead of the old remedy of sulphur and molasses, we perhaps need a good shot of Vitamin Contentment.

Our attitudes determine whether we will be happy or not. They set the tune to our life, making it a dirge or a melody. An attitude of contentment makes a happy heart. This is the ability to notice blessings. Without it, life has no sunny days.

An injection of contentment will get our appreciation system functioning again, and will rid our mind of the acne of self-pity and clear our blurred vision so we can see the wonders around us.

CHRISTMAS TREE needles are still showing up. I don't know where they've been hiding.

But Christmas tree needles aren't the biggest offenders at cleaning time. Bits of silage seem to turn up in almost every place.

Even though the farmer is very conscientious about emptying cuffs and taking off dirty coveralls when he comes in, these little pieces manage to find their way in too. We usually have enough silage specks here and there to remind us that we live on a farm.

THE BARE trees make such striking silhouettes against the western sky at sunset. At that time of day the trees look black and the sky is dressed in the most beautiful rosy shades.

You can't but stand and admire it all, and say, "He doeth all things well!"

And all His blessings are free.

Country Style

March 7, 1968

Baby...
So lately arrived from God.
Still retaining a heavenly
 awesomeness.
Little dimpled hands
Grasping
Reaching
Feeling
 ...her new environment.

Baby's laughter...
Made to tickle angel ears.
Baby's tears...
Summon an army of willing
 slaves.
Baby's kiss..
Sweeter than cotton candy.
And somehow she's sweeter still
When she's you own grandchild!

NO MATTER what project you undertake - baking, sewing, or corn shelling - it's the same story for the farmer as for the housewife. You are left with a mess staring you in the face.

Yesterday our corn pile was shelled. Today is clean-up day. All around we see telltale reminders of yesterday's project. A pile of husks. Wagon loads of cobs. It's as bad as having dirty dishes in the sink.

These by-products make luxury-bedding for the cows so today the husk and cobs must be hauled into the barnyard. The odds and ends must be shoveled up and the corn cribbing rolled up and put away.

And another big job is done!

MANY FARMERS are being real shepherds these days Now they don't just let their sheep wander in the field. At lambing time their charges need extra care. The ewes require special attention; the delicate little lambs need personalized care and often must be hand fed.

OUR GOOD SHEPHERD always gives his sheep tender loving care.

And to those who need it, he gives extra-special tender loving care.

"He shall feed his flock like a shepherd; he shall gather the lambs with his arm, and carry them in his bosom, and shall gently lead those that are with young." Isaiah 40:11

Country Style

March 14, 1968

When you live on the farm, you end up feeding many kinds of wild life. The pheasants, the deer that stop by, the squirrels, rabbits and coons...all help themselves. But you'll not hear the farmer complaining too much.

One farmer felt things were going too far when a black and white cat of another variety started eating cat food with his cats. And he soon put an end to that!

But the animal got the last word. If you happen to be driving down that road, you may still notice the animal's scented retort.

TIME is up!

That is, if you are going in the government feed and grain program.

These past weeks the farmer has been busy with paper and pencil, figuring this way and that, trying to determine the right answer. Should he go in 20 percent?...40 percent? ...50 percent?...or not at all?

He must do all this figuring using "x's" because of the unknown factors involved, such as weather and prices. He feels like he is taking an algebra test, and the allotted time to get his answer worked has run out.

Should he gamble?...or be satisfied with a bird in the hand? The farmer will probably have to wait until fall to find out if he handed in the right answer.

ENJOY it while you may!

Lingering over breakfast and morning coffee is one of winter's indulgences. Time to be together in the morning gets the day off to a good start. Then the farmer and his wife have time to talk over their plans for the day...and for the future...and to enjoy each other's company.

It's surprising how often the farmer's wife gets help with her day when her husband knows her plans.

ENJOYING God's presence in the morning, and sharing with Him the plans of the day has surprising results too!

"His mercies are new every morning; great is Thy faithfulness." Lamentations 3:23

Country Style

March 21, 1968

THE FIRST ROBIN

In Paul Revere style
He hurries from place to place,
Winging his way to city and farm
Relaying this message...
"The Springtime is coming!"

WHILE I had every day been on the look-out for a March snowstorm, who should show up but a robin? The sight of one last week, sitting on the bare ground down by the barn, cocking its head from side to side, seemed to say, "I've got news for you!" And sure enough, according to the calendar, it was almost time for Spring's arrival.

But Spring is a prima donna and adept at changing her mind. She has been known to reschedule her personal appearance before. And we must be content to wait for her entrance WHEN she is ready.

THE BASKETBALL season is over, and track is on the way. The other day we witnessed the athletic prowess of our calves as they one after another jumped out of their pen with the trained skill of athletes clearing the hurdles. Then with tails waving, they all headed off at full speed. Their "440" would leave track stars in the dust.

And the calves weren't the only ones who got exercise!!

FARMING isn't for the faint-hearted.

Many a farmer is beginning this year on faith - not sight - for the ground is like a thirsty sponge.

But we can be encouraged by the tulip bulbs that are bravely poking their greenery up above ground level. They are telling us, "It's Spring and we must begin again and trust that there will be moisture when we need it." How sad it would be if nature should give up and not come forth with leaf and blade!

THE FARMER'S most essential equipment isn't his tractor - but that ethereal quality "Hope".

Perhaps if you are feeling discouraged, you had better get busy and put your Hope in good running order before the new growing season. The best way to repair it is to review past years and remember how many times we worried and things didn't turn out as we feared. This will do a good reinforcing job.

AND A "Deuteronomy 11:13-15 TUNE-UP" could work wonders!

Country Style

March 28, 1968

The sound of the fire siren always brings a feeling of fear. Right away we think of our own homes and begin to ask ourselves questions... "Did I turn off the burner?" "Did I unplug the appliances?" "Did I burn trash today?"

We know fire is bad news for anyone, and we are very thankful for the men who are willing to respond to this whistle and rush to the scene.

When the pioneers settled this land, it was bare of trees and waist-high with grass. They had their problems with fire too. It would sweep over the prairie, mile after mile. Many things that they had worked hard to build...churches and homes...were destroyed with it. That was the days before fire insurance. And they didn't have a fire department to call on for assistance either.

MANY FARMERS got the feel of field work again during those warm days a week ago. Tractors, disks and stalk-choppers were given a little exercise.

But I think the farmers would have enjoyed getting stuck in the mud!

A FARMER usually raises animals for the purpose of selling them. But sometimes a member of the family becomes so attached to a 4-H calf or sheep...or a bottle lamb...that the animal is allowed to hang around the farm long past its prime sale weight. Parting is sorrow...especially if you know your pet is going to be butchered.

We have three 4-H sheep that should have gone to market long ago but their owner has put in a kind word for them every time the subject comes up.

And all the attention these sheep give the farmer doesn't help the problem. They faithfully tag him around every chance they get. There will be quite a few of us that will miss them.

A LITTLE sparrow is lying on the ground under the trees. I don't know what happened to it. And I guess neither man nor beast cares.

But someone knows.

Just a drab little sparrow of little
    worth.
Only one among millions here
    upon earth.
But it is not forgotten of God!

It speaks to me of a Father's care
that bottles my tears
and keeps track of each hair
For if He's concerned with
    sparrows
Then I'm not forgotten of God!

"Fear not, therefore; you are of more value than many sparrows."
    Matthew 10:31

Country Style

April 4, 1968

Going!...going!...gone!
Many little white schoolhouses are going up for auction these days. Now the desks are empty, the blackboards have no messages, the books full of interesting facts and fancy are setting dusty on the shelves. The school doors have been closed and the time has come to remove this unused property.

Progress has taken another step and left beneath its almighty foot the ruins of the country schoolhouse.

The buildings can be sold, and the land...but they can't auction off the rural school-day memories that many of us have.

One family took advantage of the situation and purchased one of these schoolhouses and had it converted into a vacation home. This made an adventure in country living for a city family.

TRACTOR CABS - the most desired item on the farmer's wishing list. These glass houses protect the farmer from the wear and tear of the wind and dust. Some of them have everything from stereo to carpet.

The farmer spends most of his day on the tractor and an enclosed cab can be a real blessing. Just as the farmer's wife would choose air conditioning so she can work in comfort, so the farmer will cast his vote for a tractor cab.

EVERY FARM has its Shep, Lassie or Rover. When you drive up to a farmyard this animal will greet you with either a growl or a grin.

Most of these dogs have spent their entire lives with one family. Beginning at frisky puppy-hood, they wagged their way into the family's affections. They became the child's companion, the woman's protector, and the farmer's faithful friend.

Year after year they performed their duties. They showed gratitude for every little pat on the head. Each dog has its own special talents... getting the cows, guarding the home, warning of irregularities around the farm or watching the children. And some dogs are just kept around because of their dependable friendliness.

Even when the dog becomes old and inactive and spends most of its time lying by the back door, perhaps has even become hard of hearing and has poor eyesight - still you will find this animal just as constant in love and loyalty. It never outgrows this allegiance to its master. It is a lifelong devotion.

THIS IS the "faithful unto death" kind of love that the Good Shepherd desires from us.
"Lord, May I never, never Outlive my love for Thee!"
Rev. 2:10c

Country Style

April 11, 1968

The willows are Spring's fashion pacesetters. They have already donned their dainty gowns of clinging sheer yellow-green gauze. Soon the other trees will come forth with their darker green creations.

APRIL SHOWERS wetting the drab earth remind me of the magic paint books the children had when they were small. When the pages of the book were dabbed with water, bright colors emerged. So these spring showers moistening our brown earth just as magically changes it to bright green almost overnight.

They tell me if it rains on Easter we will have showers for seven consecutive Sundays. If it does, you won't hear the farmer's wife complaining even if her Easter bonnet gets soaked.

BABY CHICKS...

Soft little yellow balls of fluff, filled to the brim and overflowing with noisy "cheeps".

Two small black beads for eyes and little legs, like short slender stems holding up yellow blossoms.

These little creatures look so perfect we wonder if they are but man-made toys until a noise scares them...and the resulting commotion proves there is life there. Almost from the moment they are hatched they begin ambitiously pecking whatever is underfoot.

Soon they will go through that awkward stage where fluff turns to feathers and the little roosters practice their cockadoodledoos with cracking voices.

They develop from cuddly little things into slick sophisticated pullets and conceited chanticleers...and sooner or later end up in the chicken soup.

These little chicks are symbols of Easter and are one of Spring's miracles of new life.

PERIODICALLY the mail box dispenses those itemized accounts of indebtedness known as "bills". There is the fertilizer one, the tax one, the land payment one, etc. And there are the notes about notes from the bank.

When these bills show up we become concerned as to how we are going to make arrangements to pay them. And there can be unpleasant consequences if we don't!

But the message of Good Friday is the wonderful news - "PAID IN FULL"!

"But He was wounded for our transgressions,

He was bruised for our iniquities;

...and with His stripes we are healed." Isa. 53:5

Country Style

April 18, 1968

Sometimes you can get too much "mother-ing." At least that's what one of our newborn calves thought.

Three different cows were claiming this new arrival as their own, and the poor little calf just couldn't stand that much attention. It was being smothered by love.

The wobbly little creature finally managed to get out of their reach by escaping under the electric fence and being free of them all. I think it was relieved to see the farmer come to its rescue and place it in a nice straw-lined pen.

NOTHING GIVES more beauty to the landscape than the changing colors and silhouettes of the trees. From the yellowish greens of spring, the shiny deep greens of summer to the golds and browns of fall - they all are pretty.

How lonesome it would be without trees! The pioneers experienced that feeling when they came to this bare prairie country. One of the first things they did was to go down to the river and dig up little seedlings, transplanting them on their homesteads. On many of the farms today these big old trees are still standing. Through the years they have grown from the size of a skinny fencepost to a towering cottonwood or a sturdy oak.

And how lost the birds would be! Trees furnish them with penthouses, provide landing strips for their many flights and choir lofts for their concerts.

THE FARMER'S new working season is underway. You can hear the tractors' busy noises in field after field. The first thing on the agenda was to get the small grain in.

Now most of the oats is in the ground. The farmer has done his part - the disking, planting and packing. The seeds' sprouting, rooting and growing he has left in other hands.

A FARMER PRAYS

I thank You for the task I have
Of planting seed.
Working hand in hand with You
Is a privilege indeed.
Now I ask for Your protection,
Your warm sunshine and Your rain
To bring, when Autumn comes.
A harvest of this grain.
     Amen.

"I said, thou art my God. My times are in Thy hand." Ps. 31:14,15

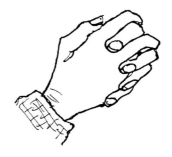

Country Style

April 25, 1968

April doesn't give us a chance to get bored with the weather. She hands out a few lovely days and then she treats us to raindrops on the window pane.

ON A NICE day in Spring you will see mothers out parading with their little offspring, enjoying the fresh air and sunshine.

If you are driving along the highway you will notice that in the pastures the animal mothers are out strolling with their babies too. Little calves are frisking alongside the stock cows. A flock of sheep has little lambs frolicking amongst them. Once in a while you may even discover a long legged new colt wobbling along with its mother. These little animal babies are very good at demonstrating their joy of being out on a Spring day by their fancy hops, skips and jumps.

WHAT A BAD time of the year for a farmer to be laid up in the hospital! The plowing, planting and a hundred and one things are waiting to be done ...immediately!! But accidents and sicknesses are things you can't postpone.

The farm can be a dangerous place in the Spring as well as the Fall, and bones break at the most inopportune times. Sometimes even some pigs on the rampage can land you in a hospital bed.

It is good that one of the main ingredients of a farmer's make-up is patience. He is used to set-backs and knows how to take almost anything in his stride. He has discovered that things usually in one way or another work out in the end.

DURING THE past month disks and drags have been awakening Old Mother Earth from her winter's nap. These fields of shredded cornstalks and worked soil resemble tweedy carpets.

Now the fields that are still dozing are being jolted into aliveness by the sharp jab of plowshares. The plow doesn't tiptoe over the ground, but leaves its footprints gouged deep in the earth.

Soft black beds are being prepared for little kernels of corn and soybeans to be tucked into.

The plowshare goes into the earth to rid it of old growth and weeds so that something better may come forth.

SOMETIMES we too must undergo painful soul-plowing before we can produce a good crop of those choice fruits of the Spirit.

"When He has tried me, I shall come forth as gold." Job. 23:10

Country Style

May 2, 1968

Pink surprises!
In all the years since it was planted, our windbreak had never yielded anything but leaves until this year when a whole row of little trees burst into pink bloom. And we weren't even aware that they were capable of blossoms!

After months of bare branches, we could hardly wait for leaves, and then to come upon trees all pink with blossoms almost takes your breath away. My only regret is that all this beauty is hid away behind the barn instead of in our front yard.

I HAVE always felt fortunate that I didn't have to help with the field work, but after visiting with another farmer's wife I am beginning to wonder if I have been missing out on something.

"There is nothing like being out on the tractor on a nice Spring morning!" she says. With the excitement of Spring in the air, and the sights, sounds and smells of Spring all around, it is good to be a part of it. And here a closeness to God overwhelms you.

There is a special togetherness when husband and wife work side by side. It can be a game as they greet each other across the field with their own unique signals.

And "turning the world upside down" (plowing) is this petite farmer's wife's favorite task!

WE DREAD to get started on any remodeling because during the process it is such a mess. And I don't think remodeling a road will be any better. Today they started work on our road and we'll just have to bear with it.

This project isn't only for the highway workers. The farmer is given some extra jobs too...like tearing out fences and re-fencing.

Our fields, yards and lawn will shrink a little and a few trees will go down...to the accompaniment of caterpillar and gravel truck noises.

But afterwards we should have a broader and better way to travel.

AND THEN there is THE Way...and it is the best! "This God - His way is perfect." Psalms 18:30

Country Style

May 9, 1968

"What's the rush?"
This was the response the farmer got from his milk cows on the first morning of Daylight Savings Time.

Usually the cows stand by the barn waiting for him, but when he showed up an hour early it was necessary to go and round them all up. I guess no one had informed them about the change in time and it was still 4 a.m. as far as they were concerned.

MOST OF all the other beautiful things in life come by twos and threes, dozens and hundreds. There are plenty of blossoms, stars, sunsets and beautiful May days, many brothers and sisters, aunts and cousins...but only one mother in the whole world.

May God bless her on her special day.

THERE WAS some sadness in this road-widening project going on by our farm when some of my favorite trees started falling.

Requiem for A Cottonwood Tree

Now I must view
Majestic, friendly you
In crude dismemberment.

These arms that welcomed birds
And shaded herds
No longer give.

This trunk, a stately form
That weathered storm,
No longer lives.

Thanks for beauty you've dispensed
In quiet elegance.
Adieu, kind tree, adieu.

APPLE BLOSSOM time...when admiring glances are sent apple tree-ward and sweet fragrance drifts through the air. These blossoms in profusion are each a thing of beauty. Delicate white petals touched with pink have the feel of a baby's soft skin.

Now as you step out the kitchen door you are welcomed by dainty sweet-smelling apple tree perfumery. It adds enchantment to our day and gives us the feeling of being luxuriously blessed.

WE TOO are to spread a sweet-smelling savor.

"But thanks be to God, who in Christ always leads us in triumph, and through us spreads the fragrance of the knowledge of Him everywhere."
II Cor. 2:14

Country Style

May 16, 1968

USUALLY LEFTOVERS are associated with Thanksgiving, but I hope you won't mind if I garnish a Mother's Day leftover with a few carnations and serve it herewith. It was too good to throw away -

What is a Mother?

A mother is a potter, molding a piece of human clay.

A mother is an artist, trying to bring out on living canvas a useful happy personality.

A mother is a physician, whose most effective medication is her kisses. (Used for both heart and body wounds.)

A mother is a teacher, teaching right from wrong ...cleanliness ...responsibility ...God

A mother is a model, showing in real life how to live.

A mother is a dietitian, laundress, seamstress, nurse, cheerleader and referee.

A mother is God's hand. He loves and cares for His little ones through mothers.

For all this she is paid - not in money - but by the love in her children's hearts and by pride in their becoming happy, useful persons and walking with her God.

HOW DOES a farmer decide when to plant his corn? There are different methods.

One farmer may wait until the soil temperature is just right. Another will head for the fields when the calendar says "May 8th" or "May 10th" - come snow or shine. My grandfather had his own method. When the swallows arrived, it was corn planting time. Some farmers get their cue when they see their neighbors planting.

And then a good majority of them plant their corn when they get around to it!

SPRING IS housecleaning time. Time to clean closets and pack away the winter clothes.

You will notice that the sheep too have put away their woolens and are wearing lighter wraps. But they don't bother about moth-proofing their old garments. Every spring they just trade their old wraps off and begin production on new ones for the next winter.

The farmers have been doing some housecleaning too. The accumulation of filth in their areas is really noticeable. They have been hauling this out by the manure spreader-ful.

The fight against dirt is a major spring offensive. If you want that clean spring housecleaning feeling, you must go over every nook, windowpane and cranny. Many times things don't look dirty, yet when you go over them with soap and water you realize how badly they needed cleaning.

SOMETIMES WE look pretty good in our own eyes, but that doesn't mean we don't need a good heart-housecleaning.

"Who can discern his errors?
Cleanse thou me from secret faults." Ps. 19:12

Country Style

May 23, 1968

"The corn is in!"

And the farmer breathes a sigh of relief. He knows he can't have a harvest if he doesn't get the seed in the ground, so he's been pushing himself to get the job done.

The freshly dragged fields have an un-mussed look; the farmer has covered his tracks. Now he looks upon his neat fields with pride, knowing that he'll have something to look forward to.

GREEN GRASS. Leafy trees. A bed of purple iris. The meadowlark's song. And the wide open spaces!

This is one season of the year when I would especially hate to live in the concrete city. Farm life and life in the ghettos must be just about as opposite as you can get.

We live midst acres of land. There a whole family sometimes lives in one room. We have our green fields, lawns and trees. Their front yard is the gutter. And there is none of nature's beauty to feed their souls. Though thickly populated, loneliness and lack of love is the common heart cry.

If we were taken from our wide horizons and cramped altogether in such surroundings, I wonder how we would react. I'm sure we would be frustrated and lose our zest for living.

Every person needs a little plot of soil, a patch of sky and a chance to be alone once in a while in order to find satisfaction in living. A plot of soil to get down on your knees in and watch things grow; a patch of sky to get your gaze beyond the earthly; and a chance to be alone, away from the hustle and bustle, so you can get to know yourself and your God.

TWINS!

The news - "The cow has a calf!" - sent the farmer to investigate and for a while he wondered if he was seeing double, for there stood two wobbly calves.

Twin calves aren't a common occurrence and it still gives the farmer that lucky "hit the jackpot" feeling when one of his cows comes with two healthy offspring.

The calf population increases in a hurry when they arrive by "2's", and sort of makes up for the ones he loses once in a while.

THIS IS the kind of arithmetic God uses when He blesses - not the slow "one-plus-one" process, but more of an abundant multiplication.

"May grace and peace BE MULTIPLIED to you!"   I Pet. 1:2

Country Style

May 30, 1968

How dependent we are on others!

This was brought home to us again this week when our milk hauler arrived a half day late. He really left us in a predicament. Our bulk milk tank was full to overflowing, and just couldn't hold one more milking. Cream cans were hunted up, and we didn't know what we would do next.

How helpless the farmer feels when the milk keeps coming bucket by bucket, and there is no place to put it!

.....where the deer and the antelope play.

While the farmer plants corn, a deer leaps across the far end of his field. This animal can't do much damage now, but the farmer hopes it will find some other territory to play in when the corn comes up.

We live on the rim of deer country so the appearance of deer on our farm isn't an every day event. But a little drive just before dusk usually gives us a peek at some.

These shy graceful creatures are fleet of foot and can hurdle fences as easily as we step over a twig in our path. Their white tails are attention-getters and set erect like stubby exclamation points!!!

OUR NEW road has taken shape. The ditches that were green with grass have become wide and bare. Now that the workers are through with their scraping and digging, the grass can again begin to come back.

Someone has said, "Grass is the forgiveness of Nature." It can be burned, trampled and dug up, but it patiently and silently returns. It is sown by the winds and the wandering birds and soon turns the black ground to green again.

Grass gives charm to the appearance of a house, and is a soft summertime carpet for children to lie on, and if its harvest should fail for a single year, famine would depopulate the world.

THIS WEEK most of us have made trips to the resting places of loved ones. Now the cemeteries are green, except for recent black scars made in the earth. Soon grass will heal over these scars as time heals the scars on our hearts.

Our thoughts, in the shape of flowers, show that these persons are not forgotten. In past days they were a special part of our lives...mother or father, husband or wife, a child that beat us home, or a friend.

We tenderly place our blooms with a thankfulness for having had the chance to love them for a while.

But cemeteries aren't "last" resting places...for one day they'll be resurrection cities!   I Thess. 4:16,17

Country Style

June 6, 1968

The June landscape has a crazy quilt design. Fields of black and green in various sizes, shapes and shades seem to be sewn together with fence-post stitches. Here and there stand a tuft of trees for variety.

Rows are emerging where seed corn and soybeans have been planted, giving a striped effect. The oat fields are tall enough to wave and bend in the breeze. The beauty of June is all around us, and we are glad that we are able to enjoy it.

THESE ARE days of "Pomp and Circumstance", caps and gowns, and goodbyes and commencements, as another section of life has been completed by many. It is time to move on to other things, whether still higher education or the workaday world.

Graduation exercises of a sort were observed in our barnyard too. With tail tassels waving, a procession of black and white calves marched in disorderly fashion from their pen into the adult existence of the feed yard. They had completed their carefree youth and now enter into a kind of finishing school.

IT'S TOO *bad that mankind isn't, freeways aren't...and rain clouds don't!*

WE MADE it!
Twenty-five years together as farmer and wife. Twenty-five years of happinesses and sadnesses, seed times and harvests. A mixture of twenty-five years' worth of hours and minutes that have mellowed into the silver sheen of a Silver Wedding Day.

There is some silver in our locks, and there have been silver linings in most of our clouds. During these years we have discovered that it doesn't take a pocketful of silver to bring contentment. It is having someone to love, lean on and share life's good and bad with. We have been most blessed!

RECIPE

Old hopes, old dreams, old friends, old joys;
Old quarrels, old bills, one girl, two boys;
Full measure of life to give it flavor,
A dash of wit to add the savor.
Bake twenty-five years in a slow oven;
Serve it warm and sprinkled with lots of lovin'.
And a grandchild is the frosting that tops it all!

All we can say is..."GREAT IS THY FAITHFULNESS." Lamentations 3:23

Country Style

June 13, 1968

June is Dairy Month. Milk, butter and cheese days. So eat, drink and be healthy!

The cow has always been considered an essential provider of nutrition for mankind, but this past year we have heard rumblings of new substitutes that make us wonder if some day the faithful cow will be dethroned.

WAIT AND SEE!

How now, brown cow (or black and white).
I've heard your moos
And could it be you've heard the news
Of artificial milk?
Said she, "As yet I'll not concede. This you may quote!
It may turn out this man-made milk
Is no greater threat than a nanny goat's!"

THE PIONEERS that headed for these wide open spaces had their milk cow tagging behind. Her twice daily contribution was necessary to keep family alive and healthy.

The cow was one of our forefathers' most precious possessions. In the early years of homesteading when the pioneer had to make trips to Sioux City by horse and wagon to purchase supplies, he would bring his wife, children and the cow to the neighbor's for safe keeping until he returned.

In the following half century every farm had a milk cow or two. A farm without a cow would be just as unthinkable as a farm today without a tractor.

But how times change! Today dairies deliver milk to farm homes as well as to city dwellers, and only a small percentage of farmers still own milk cows. But the supply still keeps up with the demand.

THESE PAST days the whole world seems to be sobbing and aching as the result of tragic national and world news.

On this June morning my heart too was troubled as I drove along the highway on a trip into town. Then my eyes rested on a flock of sheep peacefully grazing in a pasture, completely oblivious of world tensions. The unconcerned fields were contentedly being kissed by the morning sun and dew. I could hear no tone of heartbreak in the birds' joyous songs.

And there stood a peaceful little country church nestled in the farm landscape, its spire bravely pointing upward. All this country scenery was like a soothing balm, reminding me to listen for this heavenly news release...

"Peace I leave with you; my peace I give to you...Let not your heart be troubled, neither let it be afraid." John 14:27

Country Style

June 20, 1968

This past week two swallows have been staging a "fly-in" on our front porch. They are determined to set up residence there. (We went through this last year too.)

The recent showers provided them with mud for nest-building, and back and forth they have been flying, their beaks loaded with mud and grass, dabbing it on the wall, the leftovers falling where they may. What a mess!

I really felt like a mean old witch as I took a broom and swept down their labors, but it took more than that to discourage them. Maybe it is just my imagination, but now they seem to have a resentful look as they fly by, and could just as well be carrying placards "Unfair discrimination against swallows."

ALONG THE roadsides now we can spy the pink fragrant faces of the wild rose, together with wild strawberry flowers that set like white stars in a green background. Here and there is a bright purple splash of wild phlox.

We are apt to "Hmph!" and turn our noses up at these humble blooms without even taking time to appreciate the prolific free beauty they dispense. But children aren't so sophisticated. A wild flower bouquet gives them just as much delight as a dozen American Beauty roses.

June wild flowers bring back memories of little girl days when our daily walk home from bible school included the excitement of picking wild flowers along the way. There were some orange flowers we called buttercups that were worth going way out of our way to gather. But I haven't seen one of these in years.

HOW NICE it would be for the farmer if weeds would take a holiday! But that is one crop that never fails.

As soon as the corn comes up, the weeds are there and the farmer must begin the battle with spraying and cultivating. Weeds seem to have twice as much vigor as his crops.

Up and down the corn fields tractors are pulling tanks set on wheels which deposit a fine spray upon his field. To one who is not acquainted with present day farming methods, it may look like the farmer is trying to sprinkle his new corn crop. It can use the moisture, that's for sure!

But the liquid that sprays from this receptacle is much more potent than that. It is Atrazine and it is used to stop growth of weeds around the little corn plants. This is what you call modern scientific farming. This preventive measure takes time to apply but it stops many weeds in their tracks.

AND THERE is an application available that can be used to prevent growth of insidious weeds in our lives . . . .

"Thy Word have I laid up in my heart that I might not sin against Thee." Ps. 119:11

Country Style

June 27, 1968

Summer is tourist time. Many people are spending their vacations traveling and usually this includes stop-overs with friends on the farm.

Oh, the excitement of a city youngster who has been turned loose on the farm! With all the things to investigate they become so busy there is hardly time to eat. The farmer must keep his eye on them for they usually haven't been briefed on the dangers around animals and machinery.

The city boy who has watched westerns on TV must try roping and riding a calf, and the opportunity to be along with the haying and getting to ride on the flatbed exceeds any big city adventure.

When it is time to go home, the parents usually have a time talking them out of taking something along, like a puppy or kitten.

CLOUDS
Fluffy white ones that look like puffs of smoke lazily floating by.

Wispy light gray clouds that resemble dust mice being chased across a blue sky floor.

From time to time we see angry dark ones piling up on the horizon. These give us an uneasy feeling and we wonder what they have in store.

And then there are the scary funnel shaped ones that seem to shout, "Watch out!" and people try to get out of their way as quickly as possible.

IN THE summertime we appreciate ice in the form of ice cubes, but when it arrives in pellet form from above, it definitely is not welcome!

In a couple of minutes hail can bring to naught all the hours of work the farmer has put in. It is a sickening feeling to look out on short stubs where nice young plants were so recently growing. Even the knowledge that insurance will help assuage the financial pain cannot make up for the aching disappointment that is in the farmer's heart. And if you ever take out hail insurance, this is the time you are glad you did.

Because of the high premiums on hail insurance, most farmers each year go through the struggle of "Shall I?" or "Shall I not?"

THERE IS only one kind of insurance that is entirely satisfactory and that is eternal life insurance...and would you believe it, there are no premiums to pay?

"That whosoever believeth in Him shall not perish, but have eternal life." John 3:16

Country Style

July 4, 1968

A farmer is not known for his oratorical skills, but there are times when he wishes he could speak out his feelings, especially on the Fourth of July.

His feelings run deep and beneath his blue denim beats a patriotic heart. For who but a farmer is so closely involved with our native land? It is he that adds the "amber waves of grain" and the "fruited plain" to America the Beautiful.

For the farmer who works with such a tangible part of America, Independence Day has real meaning. A handful of good old South Dakota or Iowa dirt may be all it takes to make him eloquent.

"This rich, black precious soil
which my plow has furrowed,
my hands have toiled,
I recognize not only mine,
but a piece of America, costly and fine.
I hold it with reverence
and am suddenly aware
that for this men fought and died and dared.
Now must I not tend it with love and care?"

THE OAT fields are experiencing a population explosion. Each oak stalk now is supporting a family of a dozen or more little ones. And how quickly they mature. These fields are already beginning to turn to lighter shades of green and gold, which means that there will soon be a mass exodus from these wide open spaces into the confines of the grain bin.

RAIN ON the roof! Rain on the corn and on the alfalfa. The thirsty ground is soaking it up.

The sound of raindrops is like music to the farmer's ears and the sight of mud puddles is a treat. Our fields are like watered gardens, green and growing, with good prospects of a fruitful harvest.

WHEN WE come out from under our umbrellas of indifference and allow God's showers of blessing to saturate us, our lives too shall be like luxuriant gardens.

"And the Lord will guide you continually,
and satisfy your desire with good things,
and make your bones strong;
and you shall be like a watered garden,
like a spring of water,
whose waters fail not."
Isaiah 58:11

Country Style

July 11, 1968

"Who's going to milk the cows?"

A vacation isn't easy to come by if you are milking a herd of cows. Getting someone to take over while you are gone is much harder than finding a babysitter for the children. And you have no choice; you can't take them along!

The farmer is very particular about his cows, and he wouldn't trust them with just anyone. A cow can be ruined if she isn't milked on time and properly. Those with this kind of know-how usually have a herd of their own to care for.

You won't find people volunteering for this job...especially in the summertime. Milking cows in a hot barn isn't the most pleasant task.

HOW QUICKLY everything grows!

Before we know it babies have changed to toddlers, and graduate from bassinet to walker to tricycle, and feed themselves and run where they wish. Every day adds growth and soon their little legs have grown too long for the tricycle and eventually they are even too grown-up for mother's lap.

Stages of growth progress even more rapidly in the seed family. It wasn't very long ago that the corn was just coming out of the ground. Then it needed the farmer's attention in the form of cultivation. Before we knew it, it was knee-high. Now the farmer is rushing to finish cultivation before it is too tall for his machinery.

From now on the corn is on its own, to grow and mature in the sun and rain, too grown-up for the farmer's personal care.

FILL the silo!

Some farmers prefer to have their oats in the silo instead of in the oat bin. Now that most silos are getting empty, it's good to have something to replenish them with. The silage cutter chops the oats - straw and all, and leaves the field neat and clean-shaven.

Silage is just as important in the cattle's menu as meat and potatoes to the hard-working farmer, and the farmer is glad to have the silo full again so he doesn't have to skimp on his cattle's daily silage helpings.

OUR DAILY needs are provided for, too, but we are fortunate because these are apportioned to us in king-sized helpings.

"Blessed be the Lord, who daily loadeth us with benefits."
Ps. 68:19

Country Style

July 18, 1968

When the farmer goes traveling he sees the scenery through a farmer's eyes. The green corn fields may be beautiful as they shimmer in the sunshine...but the farmer is busy noticing 30 inch rows...or if the corn is more or less advanced than his own.

When he looks at spacious farm buildings along the highway, he counts the number of silos standing there and sizes up the farmer's feeding operation.

We see lovely wide ditches filled with wild flowers in bloom, but the farmer is quick to spy the creeping jenny that is growing on the fences just as profusely as ivy on a brick wall.

When we headed for home on the wide super highway with lines of traffic zooming by, I thought of the pioneer's westward journey over this very land. His path led through prairie grass and mud, while we sped along on paved roads. The miles that we covered in one day probably took months and months by horse and wagon. We crossed the Mississippi in minutes, but getting safely across that river was a big problem for him.

From our route 80 vantage point we saw very few herds of milk cows, and we had to get close to home before we discovered many feedlots loaded with cattle.

After the peculiar soot smell of the big city, we were glad to breathe good fresh country air again. And the farmer came to the conclusion that farmers all over have the same weed problems that he does.

MISERY is a tail-less cow during fly season.

We have one in our herd, and I really feel sorry for her now that the flies are so pesky. It must be like having an itch that you can't get at...only worse!

IT'S TIME to harvest the oats. For weeks the farmer has been getting things lined up. He has made arrangements ahead of time for having his crop windrowed and combined. He has hired enough help and trucks to get all the jobs done. When the grain is ready, everyone must swing into action, and it is too bad if he is short of help when it is needed.

HELP WANTED! God's precious harvest is ready too, but He is experiencing a labor shortage.

"The harvest truly is plenteous, but the laborers are few." Matt. 9:37

Country Style

July 25, 1968

Saturday night on Main Street is still a big affair. With another week of work behind him, the farmer takes time out to make a trip into town. He soon discovers that he isn't the only one with this idea. The parking places are taken, the barber shops are full, and groups of young and old congregate on the sidewalks.

As he goes about making his purchases he gets a chance to visit with neighbors, friends and storekeepers along the way. They talk of crops and rain, and he is brought up to date on the neighborhood happenings.

During the busy summer season this Saturday night trip into town often turns out to be the farmer's only social life. This is often the only place the farmer has time to take his wife and family besides church on Sunday morning.

After he has had a cup of coffee with his neighbors and treated his family to ice cream, they head for home, having enjoyed a pleasant break in their week of work.

THOSE SNEAKY milkweeds! This year milkweeds have been popping up everywhere. Their presence gave some oat fields a slovenly look, and now they are giving bean field walkers something to do. These flourish in soil bank acres and road ditches. The coarse-looking plants now are in bloom with coarse-looking giant lavender ball-shaped flowers.

I wonder if little folks still are being told that milkweed sap is a cure-all for warts.

THE SUN has bronzed our farmers. Their brown faces and tanned muscled arms tell the world that they labor in the out-of-doors.

But besides giving them a tan, the hot sun has been making them sweat. After a work-out of loading and unloading hay bales on an extra hot July day, the farmer reaches evening just plain worn-out. And there is only one place to go when you are all tired out...and that is to bed! It's surprising how a night of sleep can renew the strength and make you arise refreshed and ready for another day.

WHEN TROUBLES and sins make us so weary we don't know if we can go on, then there is only one place to go...and being with Him refreshes tired, aching souls!

"Come unto me, all ye that labor and are heavy laden, and I will give you rest." Matt. 11:28

Country Style

August 1, 1968

At the end of the day I like to sit on the back doorstep and enjoy God's world. The old apple tree is now demurely revealing little light green apples amongst its leaves. Spicy fragrances drift from my petunia bed, and at this time of day the birds are busy singing their goodnights.

The mourning dove repeats the same sad tune it sang at dawn, but the meadowlark seems to have saved its loveliest songs for eventide. And I am glad I took time to revel in the luxuries of nature late on a midsummer day.

SINCE THE last rain the pigs have been having the time of their lives, and you can see what they have been up to by the dried mud coat they all are wearing.

Mud puddles are to pigs what the beach is to people, and a pig's rooting and digging can outdo any child's play in the sand.

But no person lying on the beach could look any more contented than a pig lying in its mud hole.

BEING AWAKENED to the beat of hailstones on the roof isn't the most pleasant reveille. It makes the farmer and his wife sleepily moan "Oh, no!"...and they dread to see what their fields will look like come daylight. Hailstones have a way of leaving their mark on everything they touch.

The question you hear everywhere now is, "How did your crops come through the hail?" But while listening to the report by the affected farmer, we are also concerned to hear how the farmer came through. How did he take it? Did it make him bitter?

I suppose the real test of a man is the way he reacts when things go wrong, and sooner or later we all get tested. For can we always expect to just receive the good and not taste set-backs?

We admire the man who can still look around and count his blessings - even though his corn looks battered and his soybeans took a beating.

"YET I will rejoice in the Lord. I will joy in the God of my salvation."
Hab. 3:17,18

Country Style

August 8, 1968

Many farm men, women and youngsters have been doing a lot of walking out under the summer sun. And they haven't been playing golf! They have been walking the bean fields.

Their equipment didn't consist of golf clubs or irons, but of hoes and cornknives. (These too can make the dirt fly!) The purpose of it all was not the exercise, but to rid the fields of weeds.

The reward at the end of the job was not a neat score on a scorecard, but a clean, neat beanfield. Youngsters usually do this tiring job for monetary reasons.

WE HAVE all found delight in watching parts of a movie being run backwards. How ridiculous it looks to see people running and walking backwards and undoing what they have done!

This year as the farmers kept watch over their oat fields, they began to get the feeling that the reel had been reversed for the oats that had been planted as usual, had progressed as usual, and was ripening into a nice golden color, suddenly began to get green again, contrary to normal processes.

This strange situation is thought to have come about because of the dry spring. When it did rain, new growth developed and now all of these plants aren't maturing at the same time. I guess this is known as the year of the ever-bearing oats.

Ever bearing varieties are fine in strawberry plants. It's nice to be able to go out and pick a bowl of berries from time to time, but when it comes to oats, it just doesn't work. When oats in the same field ripens at various times, how can you figure out when to cut it without the loss of some?

"MY ROSE is blooming.
I've finally scored!
All the watering and dusting now has its reward.
Bi-colored beauties,
Fragrance divine.
Long patient tending brought blossoms sublime."

But all my rose bushes haven't given me joy. Two others have been tended just as carefully, but they seem to produce only leaves. Every day I look for some hint of a bud, but so far they have been nothing but a disappointment. Yet I suppose I will keep tending them as long as they show life, for perhaps giving them another chance may one day end in beautiful flowers.

OFTEN OUR lives are a disappointment to God as He faithfully tends and cares for us, and we are glad when He gives us another chance.

"Let it alone this year also, till I shall dig about it and put on manure. And if it bears fruit next year, well and good; but if not, you can cut it down."   Luke 13:8,9

Country Style

August 15, 1968

Animals are getting the attention this month.

These are the days of the Elephant and the Donkey. They are attracting the attention of people from coast to coast.

Citizens are watching their goings-on, not with the detached concern that they would watch performing animals at the circus - but with the awareness that the happenings at their conventions will have an effect on all of our lives during the next four years.

SOME OF our milk cows got a chance to show off the other night when a 4-H judging event was held in our barn. The cows had no boardwalk upon which to parade, but each cow had a chance to display her physique.

A pretty face or a hippy swagger had no influence on the young judges. They only gave points for body conformation and especially for those areas that showed that a cow was queen of the herd production-wise.

CALVES, sheep, pigs and poultry are in the news now that it is Fair days. Some of them may even get their pictures on the front page.

There is beauty in a steer, a lamb, and even in a pig or hen. The beauty is in the eyes of the beholder, and in the eyes of their 4-H owner they look fine enough for purple ribbon results.

At many fairs you will see a display of machinery, showing all the latest additions and improvements. The farmers are drawn to this area like it was magnetized. They are anxious to see what's new.

If you climb up and peek inside one of the cab-enclosed tractors or combines, you will discover almost all the comforts of home - air conditioning, radio and what not! It's a chariot fit for a king!

Tractor-pulling contests show the might of modern horsepower. Every farmer has a leaning towards one particular line of machinery and you will hear him rooting loud and long for the one he has confidence in. If someone will listen to him, he will extol the better points of his favorite line.

"Some boast of chariots, and some of horses; but we boast of the name of the Lord our God." Ps. 20:7

Country Style

August 22, 1968

"Where did summer go?"
Not long ago it was spring and we were planning all the things we would do as we looked ahead to lazy summer days, but when summer arrived, the farmer discovered that she was a slave-driver who kept him busy from morning till night.

Now we look back and summer has almost whizzed us by, but many farm families are still determined to squeeze a few days of vacation out of summer before it's time for school books and school buses.

"THE COWS are in the corn!"
The news sets the farmer into action almost as fast as if someone told him "Your barn is on fire!"

At this time of the year the corn looks extra lush and green in the cows' eyes, and sometimes the temptation becomes too much for them...and through the fence they go!

The farmer must quickly rush to the scene and rescue his cows from their gluttonous spree. They aren't only doing themselves harm; they tramp through the cornfield, leaving a path of ruin.

THE SWEET CORN is ready, and teeth all over the country are biting into golden kernels. The look of satisfaction on each face tells us that the smacking goodness of sweet corn isn't something that loses its delight after childhood.

The cream colored ears are well covered with silk and husk. It is quite a job getting them cleaned!

When they are boiling in the kettle, the kernels turn a brighter yellow, and then they are ready for the butter and the eaters.

Out the green husks go to the pigs...who find enjoyment in them. As I watch them eat, I can't help but think of the foolish Prodigal Son whose menu was husks and whose table mates were pigs.

But that wasn't the end! Oh, that all life stories would have such a happy ending!

"And when he came to himself he said, "I will arise and go to my Father." Luke 15:18

Country Style

August 29, 1968

Farewell, cows! For several days
I'll not be at our trysting place...
And now I ask, "Please don't be
  coy
with the new chores boy."
Take your stalls without confusion.
Give your milk without coercion.
Then happily I'll say "adieu",
for the best part of the vacation
is being away from you!

VACATIONS may be short, but we enjoy them when we may. Too soon we are back home in the old routine again. At this time of the year all the jobs are so humdrum that we dread to get at them.

The farmer's wife has canning waiting for her. She can invest many days of her time peeling, cooking, pickling, freezing and canning. Usually this produce seems to get ripe on the hottest days.

THE FARMER is not at a loss for jobs to do, and none of his jobs are exciting either.

The pile behind the barn is beckoning him, and the yards and sheds need to be cleaned, which means that the tedious task of hauling manure is in store. What is less exciting than all those trips back and forth to the field with the spreader?

There are weeds to cut. The sunflowers are blooming and their showy flowers reveal where the farmer is harboring some of his weeds. Now he must try to get rid of them before they go to seed.

Weeds keep growing twenty-four hours a day. They have popped up again in some of the bean fields, and this will necessitate another trip through some of them.

There are all kinds of repair jobs waiting. - Fencing, painting, and repairing buildings and equipment.

All these tasks are as humdrum to the farmer as washing and wiping dishes are to the housewife. But life doesn't need to be boring just because it's humdrum!

PARTNERSHIP with God makes the humdrum exciting... because it consecrates the humdrum.

"I am come that they might have life, and that they might have it more abundantly."   John 10:10

Country Style

September 5, 1968

What does the farmer's wife think of the big city?

She will admit that it is an exciting place with its tall buildings, large stores and places of interest... but she can't help comparing it with her life on the farm.

The noise of traffic is background music for the big city. Twenty-four hours a day you hear the revving of motors, as cars, buses and trucks stop and start at busy intersections. And night and day the sound of sirens punctuate the city air, as fire trucks and ambulances rush by. The clanging of the "el" can be heard for blocks and blocks.

With these noises in her ears, the farmer's wife thinks of her quiet farm home where she is able to catch each little trill and tremolo of a bird's song.

THE VIEW from a window there doesn't reveal a lovely country scene, but rather she looks out on assorted chimneys and rooftops, and setting against the sky are numerous large signs advertising everything from banks to drinks.

SHE WATCHES an apartment dweller struggling to hang up the family wash over a back railing, four stories high...where the air is almost as full of soot as of oxygen. Then the farmer's wife recalls the enjoyable times she has had as she hung clothes to the accompaniment of a meadowlark's song and where good fresh air was sometimes scented by apple blossoms or new-mown hay.

HERE IN the big city, people are packed into apartment houses. Luxurious apartment houses (for the very rich) rise almost to the sky, with uniformed door men standing out in front. The whole city is full of apartment houses - the nice, and the not-so-nice. These are the homes of the well-to-do, the middle class and the poor, but the people living in these buildings hardly know each other. Then the farmer's wife remembers a "whole" house that she can call her own, with a large green lawn to enjoy, and a community where she knows her neighbors for a radius of miles and miles.

AND THE people of the city! There are the hippies with their unconventional ways. We wonder what several months of good hard work on the farm would do to them.

People, people, everywhere. In cars speeding along, in the parks, on the beach, on the streets. The black, yellow and white. The young and the old. We look into their faces and wonder what their life is like - happy? or a disillusionment.

And we wonder how many of these people know their Creator.

"Remember also your Creator in the days of your youth, before the evil days come, and the years draw nigh, when you will say, "I have no pleasure in them."   Ecc. 12:1

Country Style

September 12, 1968

"The goldenrod is yellow.
The corn is turning brown.
The trees in apple orchards
with fruit are bending down."

As each September comes around, the words of this old poem begin rhyming through my brain. Learned in grade school, it described September then, but it is as up-to-date as this new September of 1968.

Splashes of goldenrod are brightening up the roadsides now. With blooms of varnish quality, the goldenrod sets in the green landscape like bright touches of beautifully executed crewel embroidery. Last month these were just green weeds, indistinguishable from the others... but today they are Cinderellas nodding in their finery.

NOW YOU will notice that the cornfields are beginning to lose their green-ness. Ears of corn hang in dry husk. The corn leaves are curling and drying. The farmer is keeping a close watch on its progress because he must catch it at this in-between stage for silo-filling. Not too green...and not too dry.

THIS YEAR our apple tree is going to give us some fruit. In spite of hail and other threats, it now has late apples hanging on its boughs. Soon it will unload its burden into the housewife's lap. But she knows what to do with it! She goes about this work with visions of the thick apple sauce and apple butter that will grace her table come winter.

MANY THINGS have changed through the years...but not September! She still behaves the same. And her goldenrod and browning cornfields still tell us that the year is two-thirds' spent...just as gray hairs remind us our lifetime is quickly passing.

Soon the goldenrod, bright flower of the fields, will be gone. And sometimes we must be reminded that our lives pass almost as quickly so that we spend our days wisely.

"As for man, his days are like grass;

he flourishes like a flower of the field;

for the wind passes over it and it is gone,

and its place knows it no more."
Ps. 103:15,16

apple picking time

Country Style

September 19, 1968

"Hey, ho! We're off to the fair!"

It was a lovely autumn morning when we fastened our seat belts and headed for the Clay County Fair. A soft haze hung low over the landscape, and the grass was still wet with dew.

The eye takes in a lot as the car speeds along. We enjoyed a river scene as we crossed the old Sioux River. The trees reflected in the still waters made a pretty picture. All along the way, cows were contentedly grazing. The scenes were so peaceful it was hard to believe that this was part of the same world of turmoil, riots and war that we hear about in the news.

Some old stock cows were meandering in a field, with their calves running by their sides. A bevy of blackbirds, circling in confusion, decided to have brunch in a farmer's cornfield. We caught a high school band in the act of marching, and the big tuba appeared to move about on its own two legs. Outside a hospital a man was sitting in his wheelchair, enjoying the fine day.

We were thrilled to see the red, white and blue waving over several farm lawns, and I wondered why I saved our flag only for special days. Flowerbeds along the way were especially bright now. Hedges of four o'clocks reminded me to plant some next year.

As we got closer to our destination, we discovered that we weren't the only ones going to the fair, for the traffic became heavier and heavier. We were ushered to our parking place by men on horseback...and this was only the beginning of animals, machinery and people.

AFTER LISTENING to a salesman high-pressure us about his hog waterer (it was a fine looking thing, speckled with various colors of paint), I decided to head off to more womanly displays.

The floriculture building was of special interest to women...and you should have seen the lovely table settings, centerpieces and flowers! Another must-see was the parade of holiday door decorations!

In most of the buildings, there seemed to be an over-abundance of seed corn booths. All along the industrial exhibits, the main purpose didn't seem to be "exhibiting" their wares...but selling them!

Before we knew it, we were tired of walking and ready to climb back into the car and head for home...with some new ideas in our heads, and a desire to share with others some of the things we had seen on our day at the fair.

AND THIS is all that God expects of us...to share with others our own experiences of His greatness and love...

"We cannot but speak of what we have seen and heard." Acts 4:20

Country Style

September 26, 1968

What does the farmer do on a rainy day?

It's too muddy to fill silo...or plow...or haul manure, so these big jobs have to come to a standstill.

This is the kind of a day when the farmer of the past used to fix his harnesses. It's a good day for the farmer to putter around, maybe clean out his tool shed or spend some time visiting with the milk hauler and anyone else who stops by. And on a rainy day it doesn't take much of an excuse to take off for town!

The chores are an effort when the farmer must trudge through muddy yards. He has a lot of extra work when the milk cows come into the barn covered with mud, but it has to get pretty muddy before a farm family will complain, for they have memories of days when they waited and waited for rain clouds. The farmer can buy fertilizer and good seed, but rain isn't for sale!

Even though the day may look gloomy, the farmer and his wife feel like singing in the rain because they know that these showers are soaking up the ground and will provide subsoil moisture for next year's crops.

AT THIS time of the year the farmer is just about to score. The end is in sight. The ears of corn hang in plain view. It is as if he has reached third base and now he is waiting to slide into home plate. All it will take are some warm windy days to bring him "home" with his corn crop.

THE WORLD SERIES is just around the corner, and everywhere you go you hear people talking baseball - that great game where it is a major accomplishment to hit a ball, run around three bases and get back home for a score! And it isn't as easy as it sounds!

The great stadiums will be packed with cheering fans, urging their favorites on to victory. What excitement in the stands when the bases are loaded or when someone hits a homer! But as of now, no one knows for sure who will win.

IN THIS great arena of life, each new day is another exciting lap in the life race we all are running... but with the great coach we have to look to, it is possible to come through victoriously.

"Therefore, since we are surrounded by so great a cloud of witnesses, let us also lay aside every weight, and sin which clings so closely, and let us run with perseverance the race that is set before us, looking to Jesus, the pioneer and perfecter of our faith."
Heb. 12:1,2

Country Style

October 3, 1968

Hurry, or you'll miss it!

The sumac bush is aflame with color, and the maple leaves are trying to outdo the other trees in brilliance. The Master Painter is at work. These days he is applying strokes of gold and crimson, and then he brushes in shades of copper and brown.

Each day now, as we view the foliage, we exclaim..."Beautiful!"... only to have a day follow when it is more beautiful still. But this beauty is short-lived and almost as transient as a soap bubble. Soon these bright colors will be gone as Autumn litters the landscape with falling leaves. Already the prominent color of green is passing from the scene.

Now the wind sometimes has a warning chill to it, and the cricket's mournful ditty seems to hint that winter is just around the corner.

THE CRICKET'S message seems to have gotten through to the farmer for he is busy, busy, busy! Little furry animals aren't the only ones that are packing away provisions for the winter. The farmer has been keeping on early and late cutting silage...and storing it away in the silo for winter consumption by his cattle.

One day you can drive down a highway admiring the scenery and the next day you will notice that a whole cornfield has disappeared.

THE MEN working outside aren't the only ones who are busy. The farmer's wife doesn't have time to sit around when she has a hungry silo filling crew to feed. There is morning lunch. Dinner. And afternoon lunch. All day long she is cooking, baking, or washing dishes.

But this is the time of the year when baking is fun. Appetites are good and the extra heat from the oven is just what is needed on a chilly morning.

AS WE rush around trying to get everything done, we really appreciate our good health. And this is a good time to give thanks for it!!!

"I will give thanks unto thee; for I am fearfully and wonderfully made. Wonderful are thy works. And that my soul knoweth right well." Ps. 139:14

Country Style

October 10, 1968

When someone leaves on a trip, our thoughts are with them. We keep wondering how they're making out.

My thoughts have been with five little swallows who took off for the south yesterday. The day before, they were baby birds sitting in the nest, their mouths wide open while mama and papa swallow fed them. But today the nest is empty! There isn't a sign of a swallow around. Even the row of swallows that sat on the electric wires have gone.

But how could these little ones, who were hatched later this summer lacking wing muscles and flying experience - take off on such a long trip? Can they possibly make it? I suppose I'll never know.

A FARM home nestled among the ripening cornfields, tall silos reaching toward the sky...and not far away, a herd of cows contentedly grazing. It's a peaceful scene! You would never guess that danger is lurking here.

At this time of the year it isn't unusual to see someone bandaged or sick in the vicinity of the silos. It happens every year! Gases from the freshly cut silage are treacherous and a person is lucky to come through a bout with this. And one slip when climbing the silo to set pipes has landed more than one farmer in a hospital bed.

At silo filling time, as well as at corn-picking time, the farmer has to be careful every time he turns around. He knows that these hazards are not to be fooled with.

WHEN YOU stop to think of all the things that could happen during a day's work, a farmer would be wise to ask for help - before he gets out of bed!

Farmer's Morning Prayer

Lord of my workdays
   ...as well as my Sabbaths,
Today I must do dangerous things.
   Make me steady!
My eyes will not always recognize
   dangers.
   Alert me!
In my hurrying I may become careless.
   Slow me down!
And when I grow tired and prone to accidents,
   Give me strength.
   Watch over me every moment so that
   Evening will find me unharmed and well.
                     Amen.

"For he will give his angels charge of you, to guard you in all your ways." Ps. 91:11

Country Style

October 17, 1968

Baby's been to visit.
Happy memories remain.
She left her fingerprints on our hearts.
And nose smudges on the pane.

The main course may be delicious...but then comes the dessert - that extra-special delight that was prepared just for enjoyment.

That's kind of the way life is. We can savor every phase of it - childhood, youth, marriage, motherhood...and then comes that yummy time of Grand-motherhood.

Grandmothering can be compared to the privilege of enjoying someone else's flower garden. You have no work with it...only enjoyment. You can watch the rosebuds open and enjoy their fragrance.

AFTER ONE year of living in this dimension there are many precious little finger-prints all over my heart. I have no desire to wipe them off for each one reminds me of a happiness my grandchild has brought.

The first one was imprinted the day I first saw her. I had been waiting and wondering what she would be like. Then I saw the little bundle...with tiny fingers and little round cheeks. And she was "just right"!

Each heart-imprint reminds me of a Grandma-thrill. There was the day – I received one of her first smiles, and I found that "Happiness was little chubby arms encircling my neck...and baby jabbering." I have watched her personality unfold as she has tried to communicate...with question-mark expressions and show-off sessions, and the wide-eyed excitement at her new world. She is cuddly in a nightie and dainty in a pretty dress.

There was grandma-pride in new words and first steps. And there was Grandma-fun as baby claps and bounces on my knee to an old Norwegian hymn...which no one but she and I can understand!

This year of being Grandma has been a happy time, and each new dawn must have sprinkled baby with sweetness for she has grown more loveable day by day.

Happy first birthday, little Kristen!

OCTOBER'S BRIGHT blue weather. Falling leaves. Mornings when Jack Frost's white breath is still on the grass.

Now it becomes easy to distinguish the hardier plants from the delicate ones. One touch of frost leaves the morning glories limp and dark. But the mums bloom on.

SOMETIMES the chill hand of trouble drops on us, but it need not be a killing frost...for

"Therefore take the whole armor of God that you may be able to withstand in the evil day, and having done all, to stand." Eph. 6:13

Country Style

October 24, 1968

This morning I came across a recipe for baked beans. It read:

"Wash beans; cover with water and soak overnight."

Then I looked outside at another moist day and wondered if this was what Mother Nature had in mind for our soybeans. This rainy weather isn't exactly what we need for soybean combining.

THE MILKWEED is busting out all over. Its silky insides are traveling hither and yon in search of a plot for next year's residence. Now their tall lanky skeletons are ready to be a part of someone's fall bouquet.

THESE DAYS the conversation over coffee cups have a political flavor. In fact, sometimes they become as heated as the coffee!

This is as it should be. In our democratic society we should be interested and carefully weigh the candidates before election time. We each have the privilege to vote as we ourselves feel is best.

It is a big responsibility, for all we hear are Words, Talk and Promises. The candidates just give us their recipes, and we can't really tell how good cooks they are until we get a bite of the concoction they are talking about. Of course, sometimes we have sampled some of their other dishes and this gives us an idea if we will like this one.

Then we wonder if it is only talk. A picture of a cake in a magazine looks good...but we would rather have realities!

Now the candidates are FOR us...FOR everybody! But we are looking for the ones who will be just as concerned about us and our needs when they get elected!

THERE IS one candidate whose devotion never lets us down...no matter what!

"For I am persuaded that neither death, nor life, nor angels, nor principalities, nor things present, nor things to come, nor powers, nor height, nor depth, nor anything else in all creation, will be able to separate us from the love of God in Christ Jesus our Lord." Romans 8:38, 39

Country Style

November 21, 1968

"For everything there is a season; and a time for every matter under heaven."

There is a time to sow and a time to reap.

But this year farmers are struggling through the corn reaping process. It is the time...but a lot of the corn has too much moisture for keeping.

The farmers feel almost as frustrated as we do when we are baking bread and have an afternoon appointment to keep - and the dough decides to be slow at rising! This leaves us in a predicament. Should we cancel the appointment and wait! Take a chance on baking it as it is? Or find a warm place where it can be rushed along?

The farmer has the same choices, more or less.

We have discovered that there is even a time for sickness, and at times like these, a hospital is much appreciated.

THE HOSPITAL...
factory of healing
beehive of activity
the white-frocked female's domain
a busy depot...
where new little boys and girls
make their first stop
and many bodies get back
on the right track.

a repair stop for many
...and the last stop for some.
where passengers wear basic white
   back-tied clothes
that are often accessorized
with bandages, clips and casts
and lunch on pills and capsules.

You may have to enter the "arena of
   no memories"
where green garmented men and
   women
battle for your health with scalpel and
   suture.
but you will always have the memory
   of the tasteless flavored thermometer
and the deliciousness of plain ice
   water.
Where pain is soothed with a needle
and you are pulsed and blood-
   pressured day and night.

Nurses...the efficient cogs in the
   wheels
that wake us in the morning
and tuck us in at night.
Their smiles give encouragement
their words bring assurance
and they have the amazing ability
to handle bodies
of all dimensions.

Here your eyes are opened to
   fellow sufferers
...in worse shape than you
and your heart thumps with
   thanksgiving
when health is close at hand
and you bid "Farewell"
resolving to bring cheer to others
who travel this horizontal trail.

(continued)

(November 21, 1968 - continued)

For you have learned
that being remembered
is the magic medicine
that heals and strengthens the heart
...no matter what the malady.

Through good times and bad
times, the most comforting knowledge of all is knowing you are being
remembered by God...
"Even these may forget, yet I
will not forget you.
Behold, I have graven you on
the palms of my hands."
Isa. 49:15, 16

Country Style

November 28, 1968

PROGRESS

In days of old, women could be seen...GLEANING.

Now...It's done by a cow!

The cows have left their old cow paths for new frontiers. There are cornfields to be gleaned and ears of corn to be discovered. Each morning while the day is still young, they head for another round of nibbling.

I CAME across the old picture "The Gleaners" recently. It is one of the old masterpieces of art, and shows busy women out in the field, bending to pick up grain for their next meals.

In Old Testament time, it was customary to leave some of the crop for the poor, the hungry, and the travelers. The corners and borders of the fields were not to be harvested, and the needy were to feel free to glean the fields and find food for themselves. In this way nothing would be wasted and no one would go hungry.

CAN A Thanksgiving go by without this poem?

"Over the river and through the woods
    To Grandfather's house we go."

Progress has made some changes here too. Now our home is Grandfather's house, and the little girl who is coming to Grandfather's house will travel "over" the river and "over" the trees...for the horse and sleigh transportation has been replaced by a plane.

But some parts of Thanksgiving will never change. The turkey, the pumpkin pie, and, of course, the most important part - the grateful hearts.

As we sit around the Thanksgiving table this year, enumerating our blessings and giving thanks, the sweetest picture of all will be the littlest one bowing her little head. For even if she cannot understand it all now, some day she will realize that what we are saying is not "Look what I've done this year!", but rather "Look how good God has been to me!" And a bowed head shows dependence on God!

"O Lord God, thou hast only begun to show thy servant thy greatness and thy mighty hand; for what God is there in heaven or on earth who can do such works and mighty acts as thine?" ...Deut. 3:24

Country Style

December 5, 1968

Every farm has its own Water Department, and sooner or later it gets the problems that go with it. Sometimes it is even necessary to take on the project of digging a new well.

A farmer feels that things are going fine as long as his water supply keeps coming. Out of the earth's depths must flow this necessary liquid that fills our glasses, our bathtubs and our washing machines, quenches the thirst of our livestock and waters our flowers, but getting it into our water pipes can sometimes be a costly and long-lasting endeavor. Usually most well-digging is done to the accompaniment of some moaning and groaning.

THIS YEAR turkey feathers were part of the Thanksgiving Day leftovers at some homes. Getting a live turkey ready for the oven can make a person feel like a real Pilgrim.

Being presented a gobbling turkey, feathers and all, may not make you feel so lucky when you realize the job you have ahead of you. I guess we are so used to seeing ready-for-the-oven poultry that we forget that turkeys really do come decorated with feathers.

A TURKEY usually doesn't disappear on Thanksgiving Day, but lingers around and is enjoyed for days in more ordinary ways, like sandwiches and hot dishes.

And giving thanks can't all be done on one day either, for every day finds new blessings popping up.

Thanksgiving Leftovers

Dear Lord, it seems that I forgot
To thank for all the little things
That brighten up my lot--
    a newsy letter in the mail
    a plant upon the sill
    sunshine dancing on the rug
    morning coffee cups to fill
    at eventide, the return of
        family feet
    a "mmm...that's good!" at
        mealtime
    a freshly laundered sheet.
P.S. I just discovered that it's all these little things that make my life so sweet. Amen.

"Give thanks in all circumstances; for this is the will of God in Christ Jesus for you." I Thess. 5:18

Country Style

December 12, 1968

December...when the days are short, and the list of things to get done is long.

The farmers are trying to put the finishing touches on their year's work. The corn-pickers should have been parked long ago, but you can still spy patches of unpicked corn standing here and there. You see, this was the year the corn-pickers got stuck in the mud.

Farmers have had to leave certain wet areas until colder days when the ground will be firmer underfoot.

NOW IS the time for the farmer to get an ample hay supply near his feed yard.

The other day I had to look twice at the mountainous thing coming down the road. It was a haystack on wheels! Some farmer was getting ready for the coming weeks when snow and colder temperatures might make it difficult to haul hay...and he was taking the whole stack home in one trip.

"**The hurrier** I go, the behinder I get!"

This old Pennsylvania Dutch saying is a good thing to remember on the busy days before Christmas. In other words..."Slow down!"

As I was driving down the highway, a procession of white ducks gave me the same message. They were in no hurry. It was enjoyable just to watch them for a few minutes. They waddled along to a slow rocking rhythm. Their gleaming white bodies reminded me of marble statues. They seemed content with their slow way of life.

I guess we've all discovered that running around in circles doesn't accomplish anything. It just wears us out.

AND God says the same thing, in still another way..."In quietness and in trust shall be your strength."
Isa. 30:15b

Country Style

December 19, 1968

"O, Christmas Tree,
O, Christmas Tree,
Much pleasure thou canst give me."

The stacks of Christmas trees piled in store parking lots have been diminishing. Each tree has left to help make Christmas memories in some home.

This year our tree stands big and full and represents many years of growth. Unless you have had some experience with evergreen seedlings, you may not realize that a Christmas tree isn't grown in a year. And they haven't the hardiness of the prolific Chinese elm!

The little evergreen seedlings we planted in our windbreak about ten years ago still haven't reached Christmas tree size; many of them just didn't make it at all.

As I decorated our Christmas tree, I recalled days long ago when Grandma had candles on her tree, and we would string popcorn and cranberries for decorations...and the church bells would ring out on Christmas Eve, and everyone would sing "Jeg ar saa glad vaar Julekveld".

The decorations have changed as the years have passed, but when the Christmas tree goes up, it still makes the whole house take on the feeling of Christmas...and Christmas carols.

WE ALL have our Christmas memories, not only the happy, but also the sad - of years when a familiar face was missing or we were far from home. Even now, as we look around us and hear news reports of hate, we wonder why these things need be at Christmas time. But the world wasn't in any better shape that first Christmas.

A Shepherd's Memories

I sat and brooded at end of day...
What was the world coming to, anyway?
The price of sheep
our land oppressed,
God has forgotten us, I guessed.

But then I heard an angel say,
"See WHAT has come to the world today!"
I saw and smiled
My world was new
God had whispered "I love you!"
(John 3:16)

May this Christmas leave you with many blessed and precious memories! Merry Christmas!

Country Style

December 26, 1968

Snow.

Sometimes it falls on the earth softly and silently. At other times, each snowflake arrives with stinging fury. When it teams up with the wind, the whole out-of-doors appears to be throwing a tantrum.

The animals have respect for the weather. The cattle turn their backs to the storm. At times the snow seems to lash them like a whip, and keeps the frightened animals on the move.

I looked out my kitchen window one blustery morning and could make out ghostlike faces staring in my direction. There midst gusts of snow stood someone's ice and snow-covered cattle, hovering together. Their stormy night of wandering had ended when they found a little protection near our house.

IT'S A Christmas world!

For a few days we dwell in a world of beautiful decorations, grand Christmas music, good eats, good wishes, friendliness and family. Special days. Christmas is the exclamation point at the end of the year.

TOO SOON the great day is over and it is the day "after" Christmas. The house is messy in a happy sort of way. There is a relaxed, contended feeling among both young and old, who can forget about school, schedules and routine for a few days.

THE LITTLEST one is still wide-eyed but mystified at the goings-on...of Christmas tree and packages...and the figures in a crèche that are a "no-no!"

The packages have been opened. All the beautiful wrappings are disposed of...but the acts and thoughts of love remain. The toys have been tried and some are already broken. The cranberry stains on the tablecloth remind us of yesterday's menu. The Christmas tree needles have begun to drizzle. In the corner are the packages that turned out to be wrong sizes or colors. But even if Christmas is on the wane according to the calendar, these are the days when our Christmas feelings are busting out all over. Our hearts are warm and happy!

IT'S TIME for "thank yous". As we reflect on the joys of Christmas, we wonder what was the better part..."to give" or "to receive". We were blessed by both.

Have you discovered that when you "receive" you immediately begin to figure out how you will repay the gesture. It must be because we're a proud people and don't want to be obligated to anyone.

THERE ARE times when all we can do in return is ask why "the greatest gift of all" remains unclaimed Christmas after Christmas.

"But as many as received him, to them gave he power to become the sons of God."   John 1:12

Country Style

January 2, 1969

Desserts with whipped cream. Pie and whipped cream. Salads piled high with whipped cream.

This holiday season everything seems to be topped with white stuff. Not only the food, but the whole out-of-doors has that added touch. In some places it is thickly spread and in other places it stands in dainty peaks - just like whipped cream! The cow's hay has been dabbed with white fluff and often the feed bunks are full of it. Now the farmer goes about doing chores with shovel in hand.

These days as the cows munch on frosty treats and cool silage, I wonder if they dream of green pastures and sunny days. They certainly don't seem to be very elated about the snow.

THE PHEASANTS are experiencing their own Biafra. A bevy of them are trying to nestle in a snow drifted windbreak. They make trips out to a nearby cornfield, hunting for food in the snow. It's lean pickings and the prospects of their survival are not very good.

THE SOUND of a big Holstein cow loudly "Mooing" down by the barn won't let us forget that a new calf was born. It's a farm's New Year's baby! This wobbly calf, tottering unsteadily as it tries to get to its feet and begin living, bawls for help. I have noticed that every one of the calf's cries for help is heard by its mother. She has stationed herself outside the barn. Here she can hear and answer her offspring. You see, the uppermost thing in her life is her concern for her calf.

In these early days of 1969, this new year appears to be just as shaky and uncertain as our new calf. This wobbly calf is a better symbol of the New Year than the diapered baby we are familiar with.

THIS NEW year of 1969 will lose its dread when we realize that all we have to do when things seem uncertain or our knees feel shaky is to open our mouths...and our cries too will be heard by Someone who cares.

"Call unto me, and I will answer thee, and show thee great and mighty things, which thou knowest not." Jer. 33:3

Country Style

January 9, 1969

"It's going to be a long, hard winter!"

You don't have to be a Jean Dixon to make this prediction. We already feel we've had our fill of north pole temperatures and snowbanks, but the calendar reminds us that Spring is still a long way off.

...SO lay in a supply of food and fuel, some popcorn, apples, good books and some yarn for knitting... and make up your mind to enjoy it.

WE MAY be fed up with this cold white world and wish for sunnier climes, but there are people who would be happy to be in our snow boots. This was brought home to me the other day when I heard some boys being interviewed on TV. They longed to trade the hot climate of Vietnam for our white weather.

"**HAS THE** snowplow been by yet?"

After a stormy day this is the question that is on everybody's mind. Everyone waits for the snowplow. This winter there have been many days when this big clumsy-looking piece of equipment has been the most welcome sight.

When we are snowbound we live in a little world of our own, but the snowplow is the key that opens the door to the outside world for us again.

THE PARADOX
While men travel to the moon
...I sit MAROONED and snowbound!

WHILE WATCHING the adventures of Apollo 8, we began to wonder if there were any obstacles that could stop man anymore...and we felt pretty big. Then we looked out our door and realized that we couldn't even get out our driveway, and this brought us down to size again.

DURING THIS winter weather we have come to prefix our invitations and announcements with these words..."If the weather is favorable..." We have learned that there are forces that can change the plans of mice and men, and the weather is one of them.

BOTH SUMMER and winter, as we plan our tomorrows, we ought always to add...

"If the Lord wills, we shall live and do this, or that."   James 4:15

Country Style

January 16, 1969

Yesterday's necessities are today's curiosities. The kerosene lamp. The pot belly stove. The spinning wheel and the kitchen pump. It is hard to understand how Grandma could manage without our modern conveniences.

But there was something that Grandma had that I still have a wondering curiosity about. It was her square wooden egg crate. When she filled it with white and brown eggs she could accomplish almost anything with it.

This egg container was small enough for a woman to carry and it fitted nicely in the back seat...but it held enough eggs to make unbelievable purchases.

Grandma never left for town without her little egg crate. Off to the grocery store she went with her produce. As years go by and prices go up, the memories of all the groceries she could get in return for her eggs seems almost miraculous. To do the same today, the eggs would have to be made of gold.

Grandma's wooden egg crate was almost like Aladdin's lamp, It was able to produce in any emergency. Need some material for a dress? or hose or socks? a birthday gift, offering for Ladies Aid? or liniment or fruit to can? Grandma would never hesitate. She loaded her faithful egg crate and hauled it off to town.

I guess I'll always marvel at what a paltry few eggs could do in Grandma's days. But that was long ago. Today it takes a fat checkbook to replace Grandma's magic egg crate.

THE CONTENTED cows you hear about aren't always contented! Especially these days when exposure to below zero weather has caused some painful complications. Now you find out that cows can be very emphatic about their "Don't touch me's!"

The money the dairyman earns - he deserves every penny of it. A certain amount of discomfort goes with the job, such as being stepped on now and then by a ton-sized cow, or receiving a good kick once in a while. And getting a tail whipped in your eye doesn't feel very good either!

When you milk the same cows morning and night, you learn to size them up. Some have a mean streak. Some are nervous. And there are others that are a disappointment. They have so little to give that it's hardly worth the bother. But the dairyman has some good old faithfuls in his herd, and he sings the praises of the one that is so generous that the bucket can't contain it all. She does what is expected of her and then some!

THAT'S THE way God always gives. He outdoes our expectations! "Now unto him that is able to do exceeding abundantly above all that we ask or think be glory throughout all ages. Amen."   Eph. 3:20, 21

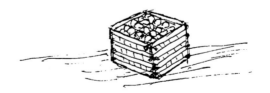

Country Style

January 23, 1969

Daybreak in Winter.

Even the alarm clock rings in shivery tones on a cold winter morning. Summer or winter, the farmer must get up at pre-dawn...for the chores are waiting.

He heads for the dark and chilly regions beyond, where his breath takes on frosty visible-ness and each footstep noisily crunches beneath his feet. A look at the thermometer draws a "Brrrrrr" from him. If he had his druthers, he'd still be in his warm bed.

Even though day seems to break slowly and lazily, the hands of the clock on the wall turn twice as fast in the early morning. There is no time to waste. School children must be roused from their cozy beds and breakfasted, bundled and snow booted. They too must leave their warm surroundings for winter's icy air. The yellow school bus will soon be driving up...and then it's "all aboard" for the adventures of another winter day.

But some mornings, if you have the time, you may look out the east window as rosy footlights light up the eastern stage, and you will be able to behold the grand entrance of a new day.

"HAVE YOU had your vitamins today?"

Some years ago it was a bottle of cod liver oil that supplied the needed Vitamin D during the winter months when sunshine and fresh fruits and vegetables were lacking. Mothers have always tried to maintain the good health of their families... even if it was distasteful!

The farmer doesn't only have the health of his family to be concerned about. He also wants healthy animals. If it takes cod liver oil meal or vitamin D shots to keep them that way, he'll supply it.

Our little calves weren't getting along very well. In fact, two of them were going downhill very rapidly. After consulting the veterinarian, the farmer was advised that they lacked Vitamin D. It was hard to believe that one little vitamin could have that much effect. But now that the farmer makes his rounds with vitamins every day, they are much improved. Vitamins really do help!

FOR HEALTHY, happy spiritual and mental well-being... B, I, B, L, E!!

"Thy words were found, and I ate them, and thy words became to me a joy and the delight of my heart.
Jer. 15:16

Country Style

January 30, 1969

During the month of January many stores have been having "White Sales", and wise homemakers have been shopping for their bedding needs.

But the farmer didn't happen to find any sales when he went shopping for bedding this month. He was taken aback at the high price of straw bales. A shortage of hay and straw this winter has made prices zoom. He wishes that corn, cattle and hogs were in as much demand.

I HOPE this poem I borrowed will bring you a smile.

Young at Heart

The morn was truly heaven;
Quiet, cold and still;
The night's snow lay unsullied
On every plain and hill,
I went about my "chicken chores",
My mind in quite a daze;
A level spot outside the fence
Drew my repeated gaze.
I looked about, I was alone.
That was beyond a doubt;
I checked again, made doubly
   sure
That no one was about;
I set my bucket to one side
As I used to long ago,
And lying down, my moving arms
Made "angels" on the snow!

The old milk cows may appear prim and staid, but once in a while they too forget their age and kick up their heels. When a mild day comes along you may notice some of them having as much fun playing in the snow as a group of children. They scamper about in "hey diddle diddle" fashion, chasing each other this way and that, until they become bogged down in a snowbank.

We think it's an effort to drag two feet in and out of knee-high snow, but the cows with four feet that sink in with each step really have problems.

Sometimes winter brings out the child in us too. The soft white snow beckons us, and perhaps when no one is looking we slide across a patch of ice, mold a snowball, or have a hankering to make a snowman or go sledding again.

THE YOUNG at heart can enjoy the simple things of life. So often age makes us haughty, stuffy and pretentious. Jesus himself advised us to be young at heart.

"Truly, I say unto you, unless you turn and become like children, you will never enter the kingdom of heaven." Matt. 18:3

Country Style

February 6, 1969

Winters can still be winters. Nowadays we modernize everything, but no one has discovered how to turn off the snow or put a thermostat on the outdoors.

We are beginning to feel like bears as we cancel activities and practically hibernate for the winter. Each snowfall makes the snow-cliffed canyons we drive through deeper and deeper. Can this be like the long hard winters that old-timers used to tell about?

We keep our fingers crossed that nothing will happen to the electricity. We are so dependent on it. It milks our cows, unloads the silage, pumps the water, lights our house, cooks our food and keeps us warm.

THE OLD TIMERS had their ways of keeping warm too. Up in Grandma's attic laid an old woolly robe that she called "The skinnfell". In her day she didn't have electric blankets for the beds, but she kept this in reserve for times when the temperature fell and the house couldn't be kept warm. This sheepskin blanket could keep the cold out of any bed.

People were able to travel comfortably even before the days of the car heater. Beautiful chestnut, brown or spotted horsehair lap robes were wrapped around passengers as they went on the sleigh or buggy ride. Instead of making a rug out of an animal skin, the old-timers had the hide of favorite horses sent away to be fashioned into handsome and warm horsehair lap robes. No wind could penetrate these.

A WINTER GARDEN

I found a garden bright and fair
And not a weed is growing there.
Come, gaze upon it now with me.
The like of it you'll never see.
We'll "oh" and "ah" at rose and bean.
Most perfect blossoms ever seen.
Forget the winter cold and drear,
The catalog of seeds is here.

First, we admire the flowers and vegetables pictured on the pages of the seed catalog...and then we desire the real thing for ourselves, and send in our order.

SOME BEAUTIFUL fruits are pictured in Galatians 5. You may desire them for yourself.

"But the fruit of the Spirit is love, joy, peace, patience, kindness, goodness, faithfulness, gentleness, self-control." Gal. 5:22,23

Country Style

February 13, 1969

The Farmer's Love Affair

You cannot be a farmer without a special love - "the love of the land". The farmer's wife is very much aware of this strong attachment.

I guess it all started in his youth. The land was his first love. She charmed him with her rambling brook and he went adventuring in her woods. He got to know her as he watched his father tirelessly care for her. She was a challenge. If he could conquer and possess her, he should feel like a man!

He soon found that to have her brought both joy and trouble. He hadn't realized how demanding she would be. But he never tires of her beauty.

In summer she radiates vitality in her green velvet. In fall he watches her with pride as she models her luxurious tweeds. Even in winter he admires her as she lies sleeping in shimmering white. But I guess spring is when she excites him most. Then he sees her possibilities and her helplessness. This is when she wraps him around her fingers. Then begins again this annual re-blooming of love. For months she will come first in his life. He will spend his days, early and late, with her. He will expend his strength on her. He will gamble his savings to feed her. He will borrow to keep her. He will scrimp and save so he can afford her. But it will be worth it all if in the fall she emerges successful and beautiful.

He will find out that she won't always respond to his devotion. There will be times when she will disappoint him and leave him with empty hands and an empty pocketbook.

He will never outgrow this infatuation. Even when he is old and bent with age, he will still get that same old thrill when he gazes on her rolling fields.

This "love of the land" is a mighty force that keeps pushing a man through thick and thin. He will spend his whole life wooing these black acres of loam.

But she will live on to entice his children and his children's children.

Valentine - Country Style

I'll not send a valentine
Of dainty hearts and lace.
To my farmer I'll transcribe
Farm symbols in its place.

It will shine with golden sunbeams
And sparkle with the dew
To tell him, "As you need these
   things,
So I depend on you."

"Twill have designs of sprouted
   corn
To show our love's vast size,
(A rose dies with the summertime;
Grain each year multiplies.)

And finally I'll be-ribbon it
With rugged bailing wire.
"May we always hang together."
- That's my valentine desire.

GOD sent his valentine - not on February 14th - but on a Christmas Eve over 1000 years ago. It had all of our names on it.

"For God so loved the world that He gave His only begotten son, that whosoever believeth in Him shall not perish, but have eternal life."
                                John 3:16

Country Style

February 20, 1969

"If you feel heaviness in your breast, find your way to a blossoming plant."

A cheery geranium with its red head leaning towards the window pane. The little smiling faces of the African violet plant. How they brighten up a winter day!

Some people have a way with house plants. Now their windowsills are all abloom. When the world outside is cold and snowy, house plants have a way of radiating warmth to a house and giving on-lookers new color to their day.

This is the time of the year when I wish that I had a green thumb. Touches of greenery around the house sort of satisfy that longing for Spring that we get now. These plants also provide a bit of excitement to wintry days by unfolding new leaves and presenting new blooms.

Even the farmer has his little container of greenery. He has planted oat and soybean seeds and is watching to see how many of them will germinate. He is testing his seeds indoors because he doesn't want to take any chances on wasting his acres outside on poor seed.

WHEN BLESSINGS come too frequently they have a tendency to become commonplace. How quickly we lose the awe of the unusual and come to expect it.

During one week we had two sets of twin calves. When the first set was born, the farmer came in all smiles..."A cow had twins!" It was like hitting the jackpot or getting an added bonus. Several days later he announced with less excitement..."Guess what? Another set of twins."

Yesterday another cow gave birth. The farmer glumly commented, "She only had one." Then he caught himself and we all laughed. Humans too easily take blessings for granted. We are never satisfied.

SIGN in a travel agency window: "Let yourself go."

I'm sure the Florida or Arizona sun must feel wonderful after blizzards and snow storms. A few farmers are able to take their vacations during these winter months, but I guess getting a suntan in February or March is something that most people only dream about.

NO MATTER where we are, we can get a heavenly suntan by basking in the sunshine of His presence..

"The Lord make his face to shine upon you, and be gracious to you." Num. 6:25

Country Style

February 27, 1969

"The more we get together, the happier are we!"

This winter when social gatherings have been few and far between, an evening spent visiting with neighbors and friends is a special delight. We have all missed this fellowship. You can tell it is a happy time because no one is in a hurry to head for home.

And what do you suppose we talk about? You can be sure it includes swapping snow experiences. There is also a lot of neighborhood news to catch up on.

We have had a little sample of the loneliness of the early pioneers and the excitement they had when they could get together with others.

IT IS interesting to hear some of the menus that people have been having when they are snowed in. These probably aren't too well-balanced, but I don't think anyone has gone hungry. Some families have gone days without milk...and others have ended up with every container on the farm full of it. You just have to make do with what you have.

ALONG THE highways now you can see mailboxes peeking out of snowdrifts. The first thing that is dug out after a snowfall is the mailbox. The daily mail is much more welcomed during these wintry days than at any other time of the year. Even if you have to walk down a blocked driveway to get it, you feel like you are still in touch with the world when you can get the daily mail.

The mailbox stands like a raised hand, answering "Present" to the winter roll call, and it means that there is someone living at the other end of the driveway.

These shoveled-out mailboxes along the highway are the owner's way of telling the mailman "Don't pass me by."

DURING these Lenten days, the cross stands along our daily path and is Jesus' way of saying "Don't pass me by!"

"He himself bore our sins in his body on the tree, that we might die to sin and live to righteousness."
I Pet. 2:24

Country Style

March 6, 1969

CHEER UP! According to the calendar, Spring is only two weeks away. To further encourage me, the Chinese Elm branch outside my kitchen window is beginning to form leaf buds.

Old Man Winter will soon have to pack his bags and be on his way. This has not been a peaceful visit. He has kept everything in a turmoil ever since his arrival. It seems like all we have been doing is straightening up after him. He has really made it hectic for the road crews.

I don't think anyone will feel bad to see him leave.

THEY SAY you should make hay while the sun shines, but I guess there are no rules when it comes to shelling corn.

The morning dawned with snow in the air, and the snow increased as the hours went by. But it took more than a snowstorm to stop the corn shelling job. After they had gone to all the work of getting the corn pile uncovered and a path dug through the snow, they weren't going to give up so easily.

And they stuck with it until the last ear was converted into shelled corn. But they will all agree, it's hard bucking the forces of nature.

"The sky is falling!"

The nice soft little snowflakes that land on the roof may not have much weight, but when millions and millions of them pack together, they can be destructive.

During a recent snowstorm the steers in a neighbor's shed may well have used the words of Chicken Little..."The sky is falling" when the shed roof collapsed upon them.

It's not fun to be a farmer when many of your livestock lie trapped and dead under the remains of your cattle shed. I'm sure he must have felt like the sky was falling on him too.

JUST AS innocent-looking as a little snowflake...or a cute little fox, are the little sins in our lives...but these too can do great damage.

"Catch us the foxes, the little foxes, that spoil the vineyards."
S. of Sol. 2:15

Country Style

March 13, 1969

AFTEREFFECTS
Jagged nerves.
Signs of strain.
The symptoms always are the
   same.
You can see by the way they feel
They've been through a real
   ordeal.
And to anyone who asks...
"You get that way from INCOME
   TAX!"

Tracks in the snow.
Rabbits' little footprints, like rows of punctuation marks (periods and colons), trail over the snow banks and run here and there across the white landscape.

This week there are other little tracks in the snow - footprints of little boys and girls - reminders of our Sunday company. These child-sized marks give me an idea of the fun they had. Tracks lead to a partly constructed snow fort, and designs made by little feet show that they climbed the yard and explored this hilly world that's made of snow.

You can never tell what's under the snow! Snowdrifts cover pieces of machinery, fences, the picnic table...and perhaps that thing that you have been looking for all winter will show up when the snow disappears.

But the biggest surprise of all was to uncover some green grass. That's what we found when a path was made through a snow bank that blanketed our lawn. Now I take heart as I look at the drift that covers my tulip bed for I know things are happening under there too.

These days Pepper walks past my kitchen window on such a high elevation that she can see me washing dishes in the sink...and there she stands and looks and wags her tail.

I think she enjoys the high places. Often she climbs atop one of the higher snow banks and sits and watches over the farmyard. The snow mountains give her a bird's-eye view, but when spring comes she will be back down to earth again.

WE ALL look at things from a different angle. The dog, from ground-level; man gets a better perspective...and then there is God's view, which encompasses past, present and future, and takes in things from a still higher vantage point.

"For as the heavens are higher than the earth, so are my ways higher than your ways and my thoughts than your thoughts."
                      Isa. 55:9

Country Style

March 20, 1969

ARTISTS in denim and calico. There is a knack for beauty hiding in every soul. We all have a portion of creativity inside, waiting to be expressed. Art isn't a thing apart, reserved for art centers and art majors. It can be incorporated into our workaday world. As we get the urge, we can add touches of artistry to everydayness.

A housewife creates a masterpiece out of a plain cake as she decorates it with swirls of icing. She makes a lowly dish-towel special by a little bit of embroidery. She transforms a plain white tablecloth into a thing of beauty by carefully pressing out the wrinkles and ironing in perfect rows of folds. She adds her touch to the common ordinary jobs. It is some of the love of beauty inside of her seeping out as she goes about her daily tasks.

A mother is an artist as she fixes her little daughter's hair, and so is Grandma with her crocheting and knitting. Junior makes the scenery lovelier when he does a good job of mowing the lawn. The 4-Her knows how to bring out the beauty of a steer, lamb or pig.

Even the farmer in his overalls is an artist as he neatly builds a fence or meticulously forms a haystack. He adds his creativity to the whole countryside when he turns the black plowed field into a landscape picture. Instead of using paints upon a canvas, he uses little seeds, and when he is finished a beautiful scene emerges.

Some farmers have more of an eye for beauty than others, and aren't content unless their rows are straight, and their ground perfectly prepared for planting.

ART IS even more wonderful when it transforms the common things into the beautiful. Sometimes all it takes is soap and water and someone's vision of something better. In our own little way we can be Michelangelos. Out of a stone that had been thrown out, Michelangelo could see a statue. When he added his artistic touch to this old stone, it became the stately and well-known statue of "David".

Art is doing your thing, expressing yourself on the canvas of your day-by-day living.

DEER STANDING in the snow make a peaceful winter scene. We have this picture on a kitchen calendar. The deer stand with heads erect, and with that alert look that deer and rabbits have - just like track men listening for the sound of the gun that will send them off and away.

The other day as I was driving down the highway I saw this deer scene alive and in color. There were five of them. These animals were standing in the snow beside two corncribs in a farmer's field. I think they were trying to nibble at the corn through the cribbing.

A half-mile farther along were several pheasants in a snow-covered cornfield. They too were hunting for something to eat. In the wintertime the living isn't easy for wild animals. They often miss a meal.

There are times when it is fun to be wild and free, to not be fenced in, but when the weather is rough, the tame animals have an advantage. They have someone to care for them. It's comforting to have a shepherd. Through good times or rough times, he is there to provide.

(continued)

(March 20, 1969 – continued)

WE NEED never be harassed and hungry if we are willing to be His sheep.
"The Lord is my shepherd, I shall not want." Ps. 23:1

Country Style

March 27, 1969

Suddenly
on the first warm day
children toss their coats away
BUT
livestock shed
their winter wear
hair by hair.

Other signs of spring are soft slush, shrinking snow banks, ruts, a robin.

AND TODAY I saw meadowlarks everywhere. The sight of them gave me almost as bright a Spring-y feeling as bouquets of daffodils. I wonder if these birds can sing their happy song while sitting in the dirty old snow.

THIS TIME of the year there are more bottle babies in the country than at any other time. Every farmer with a flock of sheep ends up with some orphans or twins that he has to bottle-feed. The sound of "baas" three times a day can only be quieted with a bottle full of milk. It gets to be a big undertaking when he has more than two to feed at the time.

"**YOU CAN"T** keep them down on the farm"...after they find they can walk over the fence.

Snowbanks over the fence lines allow the cattle to go visiting the neighbors, and have made it easy for both big and little pigs to leave home.

Only Spring can solve the problem. The farmer has found that it is too big a job to shovel out the whole fence line, but some have discovered an electric fence to be the solution until these snow overpasses melt away.

When some of his livestock is missing the farmer gets busy on the phone, calling to see if his neighbors have any extras. Or else he will have to track them down by following their hoof prints. This livestock is his property even if they have had the wanderlust and left their home...and he will go out and search for them.

THE GOOD Shepherd is just as concerned about his property... "What do you think? If a man has a hundred sheep, and one of them has gone astray, does he not leave the ninety-nine on the hills and go in search of the one that went astray? And if he finds it, truly I say to you, he rejoices over it more than over the ninety-nine that never went astray."
Matt. 18:12, 13

Country Style

April 3, 1969

Springtime is egg-time.

It seems that in the days before modern poultry care, hens began to cackle louder in March...as a salute to Spring. They came out of their winter slump and began to get back to laying eggs again. With this bountiful supply available, egg cookery went into high gear. Even now, eggs and egg dishes seem to go with jonquil and tulip time. Lent encourages their frequent appearance and Easter demands them.

At Easter, eggs too join the happy world by appearing in joyous colors that delight both young and old.

The egg is such a commonplace thing that we take it for granted. Yet it is versatile. It can be as humble as a fried egg, or as dainty and extra-special as...angel food cake, soufflé or meringues. It would be almost impossible to cook without eggs.

Eggs come in their own distinctive packaging and shape. We are all familiar with the fragility of this covering and we have all had our Humpty-Dumpty tragedies.

But, eggs were made to be broken. If they are left intact, they will only end up as rotten eggs. It is in the using that they bring nutrition, satisfaction and delight to the world.

The Plowman

There is no beauty in these fields of stubble and old weeds
And every farmer knows that there can be no fruitfulness
Until the plow's sharp blade erases last year's growth;
Here only weeds will grow.
The ground is fertile,
But it needs the cleansing of the plow
Before good seeds can root
And make this field produce.

Oh, Lord, how well you know
The fruitlessness of stubble overgrown with weeds.
You see it in my life.
Each day it needs the cleansing sweep of Thy sharp plow
In full forgiveness To uproot sins and worldly cares
Before this heart will be prepared...to love...and serve.

Both eggs and people were created so that they might be a blessing to others.

"Even as the Son of man came not to be served but to serve, and to give his life as a ransom for many."
Matt. 20:28

Country Style

April 10, 1969

Robins! Robins! Robins!
They're back again, in their same old red-vested outfits. Groups of them fly around looking for a bare spot of ground to land on.

Do you suppose their arrival with all the snow still on the ground makes them wonder if they are off schedule?

IN THE past, the fashion world has looked down on the farm family's plain attire. The farmer's overalls, and the farmer's wife's apron, which she used in a variety of ways, including gathering eggs in it...belonged to the backwoods. A farm boy or girl was dubbed a "hayseed" if he or she appeared in the city in country attire.

But this year the pendulum has swung over to country styles. Magazines and stores are featuring "the country look." Play clothes are made of blue work shirt and coverall materials, and ginghams and calicos. They even feature bib overall styles in bright prints, and aproned dresses. The look is "country fresh" and casual. The country look is finally "in".

"WITH AN oink, oink here, and an oink, oink there?"

It's farrowing time! Hog-houses are full of pig sounds. There seem to be oink-oinks everywhere.

Each straw-lined pen holds up to a dozen little squealers, together with a grunting mother, and they do all their communicating in "oinks."

The mother "oinks" are both encouraging and bossy. And there are the little oinks that tell when little stomachs are hungry, and there are the sleepy, satisfied oinks that tell that they are contented. Even the farmer can almost understand some of this language.

EVERYTHING has to express itself in some way. By sounds or by words.

Sometimes it is hard to find the right words to convey the feelings in our hearts. This is especially true after just living through another Holy Week...

"What language can I borrow,
To thank thee, dearest friend,
For this Thy dying sorrow,
Thy pity without end?"

129

Country Style

April 17, 1969

When Kristen Comes to Visit

The city holds no wonders to a
    girly, half past one,
That can excite
quite, quite like
"GRANDPA'S MOOS".

You'll find her perched on tip-toe
    beside the windowpane.
In toddler-talk she's praising,
    as all day long she's gazing at
"GRANDPA'S MOOS".

But it was a different story
    when she visited the barn.
She hugged us tight
    in childish fright.
For "Grandpa's moos" MOOED!!!

SOME PEOPLE enjoy the mud.

Along a street corner a little boy was standing in a mud puddle. He was covered with mud to his waist, and having the time of his life. Perhaps he wasn't so happy when he got home.

BUT the farmer isn't enjoying the mud. He has been wearing his big overshoes for months and months. Lately they are heavier than usual. He comes into the house almost puffing after plowing through the muddy yards with them on.

His cows look like they have black boots on too. They have to walk through the deep mud and they too are well covered with it. The farmer isn't any happier about their muddy condition than the little boy's mother probably was for it too means a clean-up job for him at chores time.

And the cows aren't all that get dirty. The farmer himself gets pretty well coated in the process of getting his day's work done. Today tractor, loader and man all landed in the mud. We were thankful that the only damage was muddy clothes.

MUD ISN"T the only thing that clings and weighs us down, leaving us soiled and dirty...

"Therefore, let us also lay aside every weight, and sin which clings so closely, and let us run with perseverance the race that is set before us, looking to Jesus the pioneer and perfecter of our faith."
    Heb. 12:1, 2

Country Style

April 24, 1969

Have you ever seen such unsightly fences?

The farmer is ashamed of them. They sag, and bag, are disheveled and untidy. Wires are broken and tangled. Some of them look just as bedraggled as a suit of clothes that had been slept in.

After getting a look at the fences that had been covered with snowbanks all winter, the farmer began to wonder if little gremlins hadn't been busy doing mischief under the snow. It is hard to believe that plain snow could so completely destroy the well-groomed look they had last fall. Now any spare time the farmer finds will be needed for stretching and mending fences.

OLD MAN RIVER...he just keeps rolling along.

Many people living in this neighborhood have just experienced many days of danger and tension. They have had to try to go to sleep to the eerie-sounding lullaby that Old Man River made as he stampeded towards the Missouri. It was like the noise of thousands of thundering hooves in a distance. Those living in its path got out of its way just as quickly as if there had been wild, stampeding animals headed in their direction.

The river has a Dr. Jekyll-Mr. Hyde personality. For months and years it had been just a part of the peaceful, beautiful scenery, and then all of a sudden it became a murdering, vicious thing that no one could control. He covered both farmland and city blocks, and made roads, bridges and fields into a wilderness of water. The river that we have been watching doesn't seem to be any relation to the lazy Old Man River that we sing about.

IT WAS a cloudy spring morning, with moisture in the air, and the world looked gloomy...but when I stepped outside, I was surprised by a beautiful symphony of happy bird voices. The meadowlark's liquid-sounding melody and the other multi-toned cheery chirps all were joining in concert. Each note seemed to cling to and reverberate in the damp morning air.

That cloudy day of birds' songs really sounded sweeter than any of their sunny day ditties. They seemed to be putting their whole hearts into it.

IT'S EASY to rejoice on sunny days, but when you can sing songs of rejoicing on life's cloudy days, the whole world stops to admire the sweetness.

"Rejoice always, pray constantly, give thanks in all circumstances, for this is the will of God in Christ Jesus for you."
I Thess. 5:16-18

Country Style

May 1, 1969

It's Irrelevant

Little black lamb...as you skip and you leap,
Do you care that you're different from other sheep?

I wonder, have you ever been teased for being dark and dusky-fleeced?
Or did you ever stop and cry because the white sheep passed you by?

He answered, while doing a happy pirouette,
"Does it matter to you if you're blond or brunette?"

OH, THE hustle and bustle of spring!
We always talk about the pressure of the Christmas rush, but this year it is the Spring rush that really has us swamped. There are too many jobs that have to be done in too short a time. Everything has piled up and is marked with an "urgent" priority.
"Hurry!...and disk, and plow, and get the oats in, and haul manure!!" Even the robins are busy, busy, busy.
The housewife all of a sudden has a hundred things to do - a lawn to rake, a garden to plant, chicks to care for, and that old institution called "Spring Housecleaning" is breathing down her neck and reminding her to get at it. Just as the robins in the spring seem possessed with getting their home in shape, so the housewife gets the urge also to do something with her living quarters. She has all kinds of ideas for redecorating, painting, cleaning and polishing. I guess she likes to be proud of her nest too.

SOMETIMES the farmer feels like he's riding a bucking bronco. His big green tractor usually behaves obediently and keeps all four wheels on the ground, but when the farmer is plowing heavy alfalfa ground, his tractor has been known to balk and rear up, with front wheels balancing in mid-air. When it gets these ideas, the farmer has to load it down with all kinds of weights. If the burden is heavy enough, his tractor may settle down to getting the job done.

WHEN WE feel like balking because the going is too tough, we need only hitch unto this advice...
"Take my yoke upon you, and learn from me; for I am gentle and lowly in heart, and you will find rest for your souls. For my yoke is easy, and my burden is light."
Matt. 11:29, 30

Country Style

May 8, 1969

Beauty can stir a man's (or woman's) soul.

This spring I think it is the weeping willow that has touched my emotions. Perhaps it's because it is the first tree to leaf-and after a long winter of looking at bare black boughs, I appreciate its yellow-green foliage.

The weeping willow. How can I describe it? Graceful, dainty and breathtaking; it has a Mona Lisa look, ...an air of mystery and sadness. Its flexible twigs move with each breeze - like the tails of a hundred kites.

Are the little green leaves that trail downward on flowing streamers its tears? But, surely, on a nice spring day, it must be weeping for joy.

THE CURTAIN has once more been raised on the annual production of "Seedtime and Harvest". Again we will thrill to this moving drama, with its moments of tension and mystery.

The leading character is a diminutive seed. It's hard to believe that such an uninteresting-looking object could make exciting watching.

This plain little oat grain has already made its opening appearance. In Act I, we saw the little seed as it prepared to go on a journey down into the earth, where it was to be confined. The audience must now wait and wonder if they will see anything of this little seed again.

Act II is now being staged. It takes place in the dark, damp ground. If this scene were visible to our eyes we would be able to watch the little seed as its small body swells and gradually takes on a new form. New lively sprouts soon protrude, and its old mutilated body finally deteriorates and becomes a part of the black earth in which it lies.

At this point, many look around for "who dunnit?" clues. They are puzzled as they see the ecru-colored, lifeless looking seed mysteriously emerge as a living green vigorous plant. Most of us who are acquainted with the plot are aware of the Unseen Hand that accomplishes this miracle.

This act ends as the minute-sized leading character blossoms forth into volumes of green growth. But we will have to wait until later this summer to watch ACT III, when this production will reach its climax, and we will be able to find out if the end is joyful or tragic.

The little oat seed has quite a role to play as it goes through the stages of germination, growth and reproduction. It would be interesting to hear its reaction to it all.

PERHAPS it would say...
"My former shape and form is gone, -- But I'm not dead.
Behold, I now live on IN MULTIPLE.
In giving my old self away, I found a life of fruitfulness."

Jesus puts this same thought into these words..."For whoever would save his life will lose it; and whoever loses his life for my sake and the gospel's will save it." Mark 8:35

Country Style

May 15, 1969

The deserted old farm seemed to have a Harvey Dunn quality. Today there was a touch of beauty in those lonely surroundings.

The empty house did not try to camouflage its age with a coat of paint any more. The marks of time were plain to see. The barn, which stood alongside, also showed its years. It leaned at a tired angle, like an old man who was bent with age. They looked sad, forlorn and neglected.

...But today a little tree had burst into bloom. Its pink blossoms softened the starkness of the scene, and tried to hide the old house's run-down condition. It was a picture worth painting.

DAYLIGHT SAVINGS time is giving the farmer an extra hour of overtime every day. Now when the alarm clock rings, it is really 4 a.m., and he has an hour's jump on the day.

Many farmers are making use of moonlight time too, by the sound of their tractor noises, and you can see lights moving back and forth across the fields, way past bedtime.

IT'S SPRING, and the farmer knows he has to get the seeds into the ground if he expects a harvest. And every day counts.

The little wild plum trees are in bloom. Mother Nature has placed these white bouquets here and there along the countryside, between the fields and by the fence lines. It's hard to pass one of these trees by without stopping to pick a few branches.

We have a bouquet on the dining room table, and it has filled the whole house with its sweet smell. If someone could figure out how to bottle up this lovely scent, it would outsell any Glade or room freshener on the market.

The gifts of Spring. Everywhere we look, we are treated to beauty: carpeted lawns of brightest green; the deep bright colors of the tulip; apple trees in bloom; little lambs, calves and colts scampering about.

But what would Spring be like without two eyes to see it all?

STILL..."you ain't seen nothing yet!"

"Eye hath not seen, nor ear heard, neither have entered into the heart of man, the things which God hath prepared for them that love him." I Cor. 2:9

Country Style

May 22, 1969

Every now and then the implement shops have to do business with the farmer's wife. Something always manages to break down, and when the farmer is busy, he sends his wife to town for repairs.

The implement dealer will discover that his lady customers usually don't know what they are buying. They ignorantly repeat the words and numbers that their husband instructed them to, and then innocently bring home whatever shaped piece they are given, hoping it is the right thing.

"That's the way it goes!"
The night you want to rush through chores so you can get the field dragged after supper, the cow has a calf, and messes up your tight schedule.

The day you sell your cattle, the price is down.

And, of course, the day you wash your car, it rains.

PRAYER OF THE SOWER
It's Spring.
Cows munch green pastures;
Birds have worms;
We dine on asparagus, rhubarb, lamb
and eat our bread three times a day.
Our world seems purring with content.
But in the distance I hear cries.
It is the hungry of the world that beg for food
and plead for help.
It's Spring
and time for me to plant my seed.
It isn't much.
But I remember well the lad
whose little loaves and fishes
fed a multitude.
So Lord, I give the seed to Thee,
as carefully I place it in the soil.
And trust that you will multiply my little
So hungry multitudes again can eat.
              AMEN.

"Blessed is he who considers the poor!"   Ps. 41:1

Country Style

May 29, 1969

The corn planting is finished, and the little kernels of corn are tucked snugly down in their assigned places, but the corn isn't the only thing that is in the hole. The farmer has been running up some pretty big bills. For every 100 acres of corn he has planted, he already has bills for fertilizer, seed corn, and insecticide in the amount of from $2,000 to $5,000. At this time, it is a toss-up whether he will come out even, make a profit, or end up in the red.

In other gambling, you know right away how you come out, but in farming you put up your ante and then have to wait.

BY THE looks of some of the yellow polka-dotted lawns, the dandelions made it through the winter in fine shape. We shouldn't have been too surprised to see them, because for months we had been warned that the dandelions were coming.

The dandelions use Communist tactics. They infiltrate a nice plot, and before you know it they have taken over completely, and another nice green lawn has turned to yellow.

    Tousled yellow heads soon turn to white,
Then become bald overnight.
But even if their life span is brief,
They leave descendants beyond belief.

IF YOUR heart is troubled and your life full of pressures, now is the time to get out in the country and help yourself to a big dose of lazy country beauty. And you don't have to stand in line to see it.

Spend a little time feasting upon a pastoral scene - a little creek meandering through a green pasture, where gnarled, leaning willows grow along its banks, and where black and white cows spend these sunny May days just enjoying being cows.

Let the relaxed living of these surroundings get to you. The peacefulness of this environment is contagious, and will tend to make you relax too.

Take a little time to watch the fluffy white clouds slowly sail across the blue sky at a snail's pace, and listen to the birds sing their morning or afternoon arias for you. This treatment is guaranteed to soothe jagged nerves and get your mind off speeding cars, ticking clocks, deadlines and "Hurry up!" demands.

ANOTHER tried and true remedy for busy chaotic days is...

"Thou dost keep him in perfect peace, whose mind is stayed on Thee, because he trusts in Thee." Isa. 26:3.

Country Style

June 5, 1969

June is Dairy month, so live it up!

Pour yourself a glass of cold milk, crank up a batch of homemade ice cream, enjoy strawberries and cream, and make all your baking and cooking extra-tasty with butter.

The cow is the queen of Dairy month, and she deserves the honor, but if you ask "What is a cow?" you would find that she means different things to different people.
...to a dairyman, she is chores and a milk check.
...to a housewife, she is groceries (milk, butter and cheese)
...to a banker, she is security.
...to a tourist, she is part of the scenery.
...to a meat packer, she is hamburger.
...to a veterinarian, she is a patient.
...to a 4-H'er, she is his pride and joy.

A city child may describe a cow as "that tall thing that gives milk", but a baby usually identifies her as "moo".

Often city children stand aghast as they witness the milking process for the first time and discover that milk comes from a cow. In fact, sometimes this discovery is so revolting that they defiantly state that they will not drink that kind of milk - only the milk that comes from the grocery store, where, they probably think it comes from a faucet.

WHO WANTS dried prunes and beans when you can have fresh fruits and vegetables? I guess that's the way the cows feel too. Now that they have fresh green grass to feed on, the ground feed doesn't excite them anymore.

It is a helping of ground feed that is supposed to be a drawing card that brings the cows quickly to their stalls at milking time, but now it doesn't work. These days the cows stand outside and stubbornly reject the farmer's invitation to come into the barn. After feasting all day on luscious, fresh green grass, the plain old dry ground feed has lost its appeal, and the farmer has quite a time.

WHEN YOU have tasted the "Best", everything else loses its appeal. It's that way with spiritual things too...

"So put away all malice and all guile and insincerity and envy and all slander...for you have tasted the kindness of the Lord." I Peter 2:1, 3.

Country Style

June 12, 1969

June has been known as the month of weddings. There are many of us through the years who chose this month in which to have the knot tied.

In the past, when people talked about weddings, they often described the process as "getting hitched." In the days of work horses this expression had a lot of meaning. Two horses, hitched up to work side by side, made a good illustration of the state of matrimony.

Some of the combinations of horses that were known as a "team" were just as varied as some of the couples who go under the title of "Mr. and Mrs."

- There was the team where one horse was willing to do all the work...and the other horse was willing to let it.
- There was the pair that never could get in step as a team, and whose pulling was always jerky.
- Once in a while you would find a pair of horses who rebelled at being hitched up. They hated the harness and balked at the work.
- But there was the beautiful pair that seemed made for each other. They enjoyed being hitched together, and together they enthusiastically got at the work ahead - whether it was planting corn, hauling bundles or pulling the wagon when the farmer was picking corn. This pair of horses worked as one, and they were the farmer's pride and joy.

And this too is the secret to perfect "Mr. and Mrs." teams - two pulling as one!

IF YOU head south at this time of the year, you can view seedtime and harvest all in one day. As you leave this part of the country, where farmers are just finishing their planting of corn and soybeans and where the oats is just a few inches out of the ground, you next enter Nebraska and Kansas, where the fields of grain stand high and are already headed. Each hour of southward travel shows a more developed crop.

In Oklahoma you discover the grain is beginning to turn, and in southern Oklahoma and northern Texas the wheat is golden ripe, and the harvest operations are just beginning. As you sped along, you could almost see the grain get ripe right before your eyes. And the way time flies, it won't be long before it is harvest time here too - just a little over a month from now.

In the fields and yards of Oklahoma stand the oil wells with black pumps constantly pumping out the black stuff. But there is no country beauty in these mechanical black assets. How much more pleasant to the eye are yards and pastures where the black assets are in the form of black cattle. And for the farmer who bought cattle at the right time, he almost feels as rich as if he had oil wells walking around in his yards.

(continued)

(June 12, 1969 – continued)

OIL WELLS can run out, and cattle prices can tumble, but there are some riches that are lasting...

"An inheritance incorruptible, and undefiled, and that fadeth not away, reserved in heaven for you, who are kept by the power of God through faith unto salvation ready to be revealed in the last time." I Peter 1:4, 5.

Country Style

June 19, 1969

Is it a bird? Is it a gopher? Is it a bug?

This spring at corn planting time some farmers were stymied by a mysterious thief who swiped the kernels of corn right out of the ground, even before they had a chance to grow. In some places, these members of the wildlife family made such a big haul that the farmer had to do some replanting.

When you live in wildlife country, you aren't too surprised when animals or pheasants drop by for lunch. One farmer every year plants a little patch of corn just for the deer. He might just as well, they would probably eat it up anyway.

IT'S HAY days!
You can tell by the special smell of new-mown alfalfa in the air, and you can tell by the little bits of alfalfa that have been trailing along into the house during this past week.

IF A FARMER of fifty years ago could see the curved, winding rows of corn on contoured land, he would probably slowly shake his head and mutter a hopeless "Uff da!"

In the past, the idea of good farming consisted of "the straighter the row, the better", and it was necessary that they be straight if they were to be cross-cultivated.

Contour farming would look foolish, high falutin and new-fangled to the farmer of yesterday until the reasons for this kind of farming were explained, and then I'm sure he'd agree that the farmer of today is wise in using this method where needed.

By following the contour of the land, and running the rows around hills and slopes, wash-outs are prevented and the soil and moisture are held where they belong.

And he'd have to admit that these curved rows can be beautiful too.

SOMETIMES our lives follow such confusing, puzzling paths that we too may moan "Uff da!", and wonder what good can come of such a complicated mess, but some day later we will look back on it and see that there was a purpose in this crooked design, and afterwards it will even look beautiful to us because then we will be able to see the reason for it all.

"For we know that all things work together for good to those who love God."   Romans 8:28

Country Style

June 26, 1969

Both the housewife and the farmer will agree that if it weren't for weeds and dust, life would be much easier.

When the housewife sees a film of dust on her furniture, she grabs a dustcloth and gets busy. She isn't satisfied until the rich brown tones of the wood shine through and her house looks spic and span.

When the farmer notices that the spaces between his corn rows are turning a dirty green, it's time to jump on his cultivator and get his cornfield tidied. As his tractor and cultivator go down the rows, the deep brown shades of mother earth appear in sharp contrast to the green rows of corn, and his field takes on a neat look.

To both housewife and farmer, the satisfaction of a job well done is labor's reward.

THIS IS the time of roses and daisies. You will find them in well-tended gardens and peeking at you from roadside ditches. Both kinds give enjoyment.

In this "hurry up" age of instant coffee and instant potatoes, we want our enjoyment right now. We haven't time to wait for coffee to perk or potatoes to boil, or even for a flower seed to grow. This "right now" principle has even gone over into our gardening.

Now we go to town and pick up flowers, instead of seeds. The petunias, marigolds, and even the rose bushes are already in bloom when we buy them, and all we have to do is take them home, dig a hole for them and keep them weeded and watered. We have our pretty blossoms but we have missed out on the excitement and anticipation that goes with growing flowers from seed.

The process of growing a flower from seed is a long one, but it leaves a person with a feeling of accomplishment and pride which purchasing flowering plants cannot give. We plant a seed, then check the spot each day for signs of life. We experience a thrill when the first shoot appears. Carefully we weed and water and watch its progress with a feeling of expectancy, always waiting for the first bud and the first blossom. A thing of beauty is worth waiting for.

WAITING is never hard when there is something rewarding at the end...

"Behold, the farmer waits for the precious fruit of the earth, being patient over it until it receives the early and the late rain. You also be patient. Establish your hearts, for the coming of the Lord is at hand."

James 5:7, 8

Country Style

July 3, 1969

Ingredients for a Great America

Four things in any land must
   dwell.
If it endures and prospers well:
One is manhood true and good:
One is noble womanhood;
One is child life, clean and bright;
And one an altar kept alight.

Author Unknown

THESE ARE the same four ingredients that go into a family farming operation. The farmer, his wife and his children, all have their bit to contribute. To make a success of it, each must do his best. And the incentive behind it all is the same - the desire to keep it a place of which to be proud.

The farmer, if he is a good husbandman, farms according to what is good for his land, his animals, and his family. He is humble enough not to be ashamed of work, sweat or overalls, and courageous enough not to let weeds, prices or long hours scare him out; kind enough to care for the smallest little pig or orphan lamb; and wise enough to do his best and leave the rest to his God.

The farmer's wife has an important role to play. Besides preparing the food that keeps the hard-working crews going, and filling in where needed, it is her job to bring out the better qualities in them. She must teach cleanliness...even though they must work with dirt. She must teach manners...even though their labor is rough and tough. She must teach the necessity of folded hands, as well as calloused hands.

The children have their part to contribute - running errands, caring for animals, and that hot, tiresome task of walking the beans, while at the same time learning the lifetime lessons of responsibility, dependability, helping others, and of not being afraid of work.

A farm home knows the reality of God, for it sees the sun faithfully rise each morning, and this home is set in green surroundings where bits of Garden of Eden blessings brighten up each day with bird songs, fragrant flowers and beautiful sunsets, and where almost every day miracles in the form of baby animals and growing seeds can be witnessed first hand. The hearts of the farm family are the altars where daily offerings of thanksgiving are made.

Family farming is Father, Mother, brother, sister and God all joining together in the project of growing crops, animals and people, and experiencing love while doing it.

Family farms help make America GREAT. They not only produce food for the nation's tables, but they produce young men and women who make good Americans.

Prayer for America

Dear Lord,
Keep us ware of the fact that the greatness of America does not depend on its wealth, its military power, its population, or its educational systems.

But on the character of its men, women and children. And on their relationship with Thee. Amen.

Micah 6:8

Country Style

July 10, 1969

WHERE DID THE BABY GO?

It seems but just a little while
we listened to a baby's "goos"
and coaxed a baby's smile.
Now her laughs come naturally
and she holds conversations with
   me.
Her bottles have been put away;
a fork and spoon are here to stay.
Now her rattle she's forsook
and plays with dolls and picture
   books.
Tiny bootees have been replaced
by little red tennis shoes, all laced.
Behold, an energetic missy
now replaces baby Krissy.

CHILDREN change so rapidly. In between visits you discover that baby has changed to toddler, and a little boy or girl has changed into a teenager...and the new grandchild has changed into an interesting little granddaughter.

Everything changes rapidly. While the farmer has been busy planting and cultivating corn, his oat field has taken on a new look. It doesn't seem long ago that the oats field was only a few inches high. Now it has already headed with new little oat grains and matured into another stage of its development. It's hard to keep up with the growing spurts of either crops or children.

CATTLE NEED sidewalks too.
Along feed bunks and hay-feeders where animal feet make many trips everyday, mud holes soon develop. And who likes to stand knee-deep in mud and eat? The farmer has just laid a section of cement by his hay feeder. Now rain or shine, the milk cows can stand on solid ground and eat their hay.

SOLID GROUND has been provided for us too...

"He drew me up from the desolate pit, out of the miry bog, and set my feet upon a rock, making my steps secure."   Ps. 40:2

Country Style

July 17, 1969

The fields have been so quiet lately that a person might assume that all the farmers had gone fishing.

The farmer has to adjust his work schedule to accommodate the whims of the weather. Now when his fields are off limits to big heavy tractors because they are in a rice paddy condition, the farmer busies himself with fencing and repair jobs that have been waiting for him.

SUMMERTIME is vacation time for most city people, when many of them look forward to a visit on the farm. It's good to get away from the city noises and wake up to the sound of bird songs and inhale good fresh air, instead of soot-tainted atmosphere, and to gaze on peaceful green fields and trees, instead of the hot concrete of the city.

Here their children are content to lean on the fence and watch the antics of calves and pigs as they eat and play; the TV has no interest for them when the adventure of the outdoors calls. When there are real animals around, the stuffed dogs and plastic animals lose their fascination.

And when real live puppies snuggle up to you and tag along wherever you go, no person - either young or old, can help but be captivated by them.

THE LIFE of a seed doesn't always have a happy ending. The corn and soybeans had been growing according to expectations, and the farmers had been watching their fields with pride. Their hopes for a good harvest were getting higher and higher. Then it happened! Like an assault of cannon fire, hailstones bombarded certain areas and left many fields of corn and soybeans in ruins. These plants had been struck down suddenly before they had a chance to reach maturity.

WE MUST sympathize with farmers whose investments of seed corn, soybeans, fertilizer and hours and hours of work and expense within a few minutes disappeared like the melting hailstones. But worst of all, his dream of a good harvest now lies shattered in these ruins.

The farmers who have had to go through this Job-experience wonder where to go from here. The joy of farming has vanished, and in some instances, rebellion, bitterness, discouragement and disappointment have taken over. And who can blame them?

But there still are many farmers who say with Job...

"Shall we receive good at the hands of God, and shall we not receive evil?"   Job 2:10

The Lord gave, and the Lord has taken away; blessed be the name of the Lord."   Job 1:21

Country Style

July 24, 1969

Green is the color of summer. Our green acres now are a variegated color which ranges from the healthy dark green of the cornfields to the rue green of alfalfa and pasture lands, and then fading into the light green of ripening oat fields, which grow paler with each day.

The lawns are bright green, and the trees are dressed in various hues of green. Even the little apples growing on the trees are green.

This year is over half gone, and from now on the golden shades of autumn will begin to show up here and there just as surely as gray hairs begin to gradually take over when life is half spent.

THERE IS so much activity on the farm now that it is almost like a three-ring-circus. In one field you will see a group of troopers of assorted sizes parading up and down the beanfield rows. In another field, muscular figures juggle hay bales, and in still another area you can watch a magic weed disappearing act as the farmer sprays his fields with 2-4-D. Noisy wagons passing the house on their way from the field to the silo announce oat silo-filling just as certainly as the calliope tells it's circus time.

Farm life even has the hurried tempo of the circus. Everyone seems on the run. We watch all the activity with as much tenseness as we do when we follow an aerial artist as he attempts to outwit nature's force of gravity. We hope the farmer is quick enough to come out winner in his race against the forces of nature too for these are waiting to grab his hay and oat crops by means of bad weather or over maturity.

CORN WEATHER.
The sun shines bright on the old farm home...and you can feel its leftover heat all through the night.

We haven't been having the best temperatures for a good night's rest, but we are happy that the corn isn't resting either. It has been growing both day and night, and stretching up in fine shape.

SOUL GROWTH requires "round-the-clock" attention too...

"Yet day by day the Lord also pours out His steadfast love upon me, and through the night I sing His songs and pray to God who gives me life."   Ps. 42:8

Country Style

July 31, 1969

Tassels on the corn.

Oats in the windrow.

...and the sweet corn season is just around the corner. There is plenty to do, and a lot to look forward to.

REMEMBER THE threshing days of years ago? Wasn't the weather hotter then? The kitchen certainly was, where the old cook stove went full blast all forenoon, as pies were baked and food prepared so that a big dinner could be set on the table. After the threshing crew of ten to fifteen men had finished their noon meal, they would head outside to find a spot in the shade and maybe catch forty winks before it was time for the teams and hayracks to get lined up and going again.

In those days the men enjoyed a long noon hour. They usually had to eat in shifts, which took more time, and also, it was necessary to give the horses time to rest. Down south of the border this period between noon and afternoon is known as "siesta time."

Now in the busy Midwest, the farmers seem to be living at a faster pace. They don't have much time for after dinner resting...for work is waiting, and the tractors are always ready to go. Still, on extra-hot days, where there is air conditioning, I'm sure the men are sometimes reluctant to leave their cool noon environment.

But siesta time hasn't gone out of style in the hog yard. Here, at midday, when the sun beats down in all its heat, you won't find any activity. If you go investigating, you will discover that all of the hogs are stretched out in a shady place, side by side, and fast asleep. Pigs always take advantage of siesta time.

SOME DAYS are "blah" days. Other days you can meet the new day with enough enthusiasm to accomplish a week's work, then along comes a day when you have no zip or "get up and go" and you must push yourself through the morning.

The cows seem to have their good days and their bad days too. Some mornings their walk out to pasture appears to be a burdensome trek, and their temperaments are anything but contented. Other days, it lightens our own hearts as we watch them go merrily on their daily journey, sometimes kicking up a heel in a "It's great to be alive!" gesture.

BUT ISN'T IT wonderful that God's love follows us through both good days and "Blah" days?
"I have loved you with an everlasting love; therefore I have continued my faithfulness to you."
Jer. 31:3

Country Style

August 7, 1969

Space ships and blast-offs. Men walking on the moon. Weightlessness and voices from outer space.

We wonder if we are dreaming...or if it is really real.

After seeing pictures of the bare, uninviting moon, I have been appreciating my world of grass and trees...of crops and flowers.

My patch of old-fashioned pink petunias is now a riot of color. I sit on the back porch-step with a contented "earth" feeling and enjoy their spicy fragrance. The elegant gladiolas also are in bloom. And I must consider the lilies that God has clothed in such pretty bright oranges and yellows so that this world would be a lovelier place.

Who wants to trade all this for the drab moon?

WE MAY hear monkeys chatter and mice "squeak" as we watch future space adventures on TV, but we will never hear any "cocka-doodle-doos."

A Michigan State University poultry expert reported that space travel is not for the chicken. Its drinking system would not work with weightlessness.

There probably won't only be earthbound poultry, for many of us may also be "chickens" when it comes to space travel.

"**THE** gobble-uns will get you, if you don't watch out!"

When farmers gather together, you'll hear them talking in scary "Orphan Annie" tones about the armyworms "that'll get you, if you don't watch out!"

Goblins may send the shivers up and down a child's spine, but these days it is a worm that has put the farmer in a panic. These green creatures give him bad dreams at night, and make him live with the dread of waking up some morning to discover that one of his fields has been snatched away.

Armyworms have some goblin characteristics. They do their damage at night, and they are very elusive and hard to find in the light of day. But you can't laugh the armyworm away, for here and there you will find proof of the damage he has done. They are sneaky creatures who use guerilla warfare tactics; you don't know where they will strike next.

Farmers are armed with insecticides and are vigilant - always on the watch for the armyworm's whereabouts, and determined to destroy them before too much damage is done.

VIGILANCE is also required in another area of our lives...

"Be sober, be watchful. Your adversary the devil prowls around like a roaring lion, seeking someone to devour." I Pet. 5:8

Country Style

August 14, 1969

Biting into hot buttery corn on the cob is a treat that doesn't lose its delight with the years.

The little fellow who is hardly old enough to hold an ear of corn in his hands enjoys it. The prim sophisticate resorts to this undignified way of eating because of the joy of it. And the old man patiently struggles with it, and feels it's worth the effort. The look on all the faces is the same happy satisfied expression.

It's messy! And it's fattening! But both young and old will agree that the tastiness of sweet corn far outweighs its disadvantages. Each year we find ourselves looking forward to sweet corn days.

Eating corn on the cob is one "do it yourself" project that you want to do for yourself. It loses something when the process of taking it off the cob has been done by the housewife. It just doesn't taste the same then.

EACH YEAR the farmer dreams the impossible dream of sailing through the busy harvest and corn-picking seasons without a setback. But few ever get to experience the full cooperation of both weather and machinery.

What is so frustrating as a break-down during a busy season? While the crop waits to be harvested the farmer goes through the painstaking task of dismantling, unscrewing and hunting up the source of trouble. Then he perhaps has to make several trips to some far off place for repairs. While he is in the process of fixing and fussing, his ulcers act up and his patience wears thin. About this time the farmer begins to wonder if he should junk the old machine and be rid of the trouble forever. But who can afford new machinery these days?

There does come a point in the life of every machine when it doesn't pay to keep patching and repairing, and the farmer is farther ahead when he admits it and either trades it in for new, or hires these jobs done.

THERE COMES a time in our lives too when we discover that it is better to give up and junk our old ways for the NEW...

"Therefore if any man be in Christ, he is a new creature; old things are passed away; behold, all things are become new." II Cor. 5:17

Country Style

August 21, 1969

Now a straw stack is almost as hard to find as a needle in a haystack. Straw stacks vanished with the threshing machine. These days the farmers are busy packaging their straw into neat bales, which makes for easier handling and transporting.

But Grandpa had other uses for his straw. These straw-stack structures provided shelter for his animals. The extra pile was their "hangout". There was something cozy about a straw stack. Here the animals gathered, relaxed on straw bedding, munched on straw, and were given protection from the cold winter winds. These are things that a stack of hard bales cannot provide.

"Country Cooking". I suppose if there was one requirement for a farmer's wife, it would be that she must be able to cook. There will be times when she feels like she is running a restaurant.

Her dinners are no tie and tails affairs. The places around her table are filled with overall-ed men. And her food is not the dainty variety. She must fill them up with substantial meat, potato and pie foods...and she usually has the trimmings to go with them.

Farm women have a reputation to live up to. The women of past generations have made people come to expect a lot from "country cooking."

There is a cartoon in the August McCall's magazine that will give farm wives a chuckle. A farm woman is entertaining her city cousins and as she brings them into the dining room where the table is just weighed down with good foods, she solemnly says..."I hope you folks don't mind simple country cooking."

LITTLE FARM cooks have been busy this summer too. They have been perfecting their recipes for banana bread, brownies and chocolate cake so they could have a chance to bring home blue ribbons from Achievement Days.

The experience was good, and the days of experimenting furnished the family with lunches. These girls may be the women who will be putting country cooking on the farm tables of tomorrow.

The Good Shepherd also says "Vaer saa god!" (Help yourself!)
"Thou preparest a table before me in the presence of my enemies; thou anointest my head with oil, my cup overflows."   Ps. 23:5

Country Style

August 28, 1969

During the summer all the spring babies have been growing by leaps and bounds. Baby pigs are beginning to resemble their mothers. The stock calves have gotten too big to be lunching at mama's side. The lambs have outgrown their baby ways. And you can hardly believe that the sophisticated white pullets were once fluffy yellow baby chicks. What a difference a summer can make!

Now as mothers begin getting school clothes lined up they discover that their youngsters have been growing this summer too. The sun and fresh air and good appetites have added inches and pounds, so larger sizes are required.

ONE EVENING towards dusk we came upon a deer and her fawn. They stood like statues, hoping that they were unnoticed. This baby too had grown up this summer. We could tell that as they bounded off, for that youngster could already travel as fast as its mother.

The baby birds have outgrown their nests. In one summer they have reached maturity. Now they are getting around in the air just like the other birds.

Our children too outgrow our nests. We look forward to summers when they and their families head home for a visit.

ANIMALS AND children aren't all that have been growing this summer. The sunflowers have stretched up higher than any of their surroundings, and now they are blooming their yellow heads off. The farmer is on the warpath, and will try to get rid of them before they go to seed.

TO A SUNFLOWER

"I must admit you are a pretty
    thing -
Your cheery face of brightest gold
    is easy to admire;
But yet, I dare not call you
    "flower",
Because, in fact, I know you are a
    weed and seek to overpower
    my fields and choke my crops.
Yes, you must go!
And I will plow and dig and hoe
Until my fields are rid of all your
    ragged leaves and flashy
    blooms.
It is important that my corn and
    beans be undisturbed.
So they may yield a hundred-
    fold."

SOMETIMES sins too are pleasant looking things, and harmless, so we think, until they are full-grown, and then they make our lives a sunflower jungle, devoid of fruit.

"And as for what fell among the thorns, they are those who hear, but as they go on their way they are choked by the cares and riches and pleasures of life, and their fruit does not mature."   Luke 8:14

Country Style

September 4, 1969

The holiday is over and it's time to get down to business again. The youngsters have had to change their getting-up habits in order to make their early morning rendezvous with the yellow school bus. One by one they get aboard, taking their books and their youthful energy and fun with them.

During this first week of school, home just isn't the same, and I'm sure many mothers are trying to get adjusted to the change as Luella Johnson brings out in her poem...

SEPTEMBER SONG
When spring is at its muddiest
The rocking bus disgorges
A horde of young humanity,
Of yelling Janes and Georges.
Upon the fresh-waxed kitchen floor
The children lope and shout,
"Oh, Mother, I'm so glad, aren't you?
It's June - and school is out!"

But time runs out. The yellow bus
Rolls down the road again,
With brand new clothes and sober mien
The kids embark - and then...
In Mother's province silence reigns,
Upon the lawn - no riot.
Despite this peace, Mom drops a tear -
"Now the place is just too quiet!"

THE CORNFIELDS stand green and tall, and peeking out everywhere are new ears of corn, proof that these green factories have been quietly manufacturing their products this summer. We must admire the efficient way each ear is wrapped, and admit that no man-made packaging machine could have done it so wisely and neatly.

Each giant stalk has far outgrown man's stature. We stand back and marvel at this field of healthy growth, and we remember that it all started with little kernels. As a breeze blows across the field, the leaves of corn violently move as if they were clapping in applause at such wonders, and we notice that all the tassels are pointing heavenward. In their quiet way they are trying to draw our attention to the One who created it all.

And man who has been given heart and brains, and a voice to speak and sing, and knees that can kneel in worship can join with all Nature...and with the stars that twinkle their praises to the great Creator and King.

"For you shall go out in joy and be led forth in peace;
the mountains and the hills before you shall break forth into singing;
and all the trees of the field shall clap their hands."   Isa. 55:12

Country Style

September 11, 1969

The fairs are over, and it's time to make plans concerning the future of the pet calf, lamb, or hog. After spending a year caring for an animal, a feeling of pride and attachment develops.

Raising 4-H animals may be a business, but along with the check goes a little heartache. The 4-Her feels like a Judas when his animal looks at him with trusting eyes as they load it up for market. It happens every year. Gladys Romedahl says it so well...

> "Your job will turn to grief
> when little calves turn to beef.
> Though little pigs are lots of fun,
> before they're grown, their lives are done.
> Upon the menu, with the ham
> is featured last spring's frisky lamb.
> And fluffy chicks, most certainly
> end up in someone's fricassee.
> Permit me than to raise my voice
> and pray you make a different choice...
> Since all of these get eaten up,
> better love a kitten! or a pup!"

WE EAT what we can, and what we can't eat, we can. These are days of canning and freezing. We reap the residue of the garden - the tomatoes and the cucumbers - and turn them into winter fare.

If you have your own apple tree, you have probably been eating apples three times a day. The windfalls have been going into pies, cakes, breads, salads, etc., but now it's time to get the rest into jars of apple sauce and apple butter.

Everyone's busy making the most of what is on hand, with an eye to future days. We follow the wise ways of the ant and the squirrel who have been laying up food for winter too.

The farmer has also been laying away supplies for winter. The barn is full of hay and the silo will soon be a giant fruit jar packed with silage preserves. If we want future treasures, now is the time to be storing them away.

IT IS possible to not only fill our cellar and barn with treasures for future enjoyment, but we can also lay up treasures in heaven!

"Don't store up your profits here on earth, where they erode away, and can be stolen!

But store them in heaven, where they never lose their value, and are safe from thieves!"

Matt. 6:19, 20 (Living Gospels)

Country Style

September 18, 1969

September - that magic month which holds both the leftovers of summer and the first inklings of fall. Some days are warm. Some are cool. September tries to please everyone.

September has her own background music. Spring may have her meadowlark's songs, but September has her Cricket's Chorus. Late on a September afternoon they give a mass concert. As you listen to their monotone chirping, it is hard to decide whether they are singing a sad farewell to summer, or trying to encourage one another to buck up with their "cheer-ups!"

The petunias and marigolds of summer still bloom on, but the fall mums are beginning to make their appearance. September's own flower - the goldenrod - is blooming in clumps along the ditches and uncultivated areas. By sound and sight each day tries to remind us of her presence and to entice us to take time out to enjoy her short sweet visit.

THE FARMER'S fields and pastures are beginning to blossom with new faces - of the Angus, Hereford, Shorthorn variety. Some of these calves are really "wild flowers", for when they have just been transplanted from range country, they have quite an adjustment to make.

THESE DAYS the farmer isn't always glued to his tractor seat. You may see him perched on top of the barn or hoghouse, hammer in hand, replacing shingles. Or high on a ladder, wielding a paint brush. Maybe you will catch him playing the role of a carpenter as he fixes the siding on a building or puts new hinges on the barn door.

The farmer has to be a jack-of-all-trades in order to keep his property in shape. There is always something to fix. These are his possessions, and he doesn't want to see them get run-down.

GOD DOESN'T neglect his property either. He keeps repairing, transforming and correcting...

"And I am sure that He who began a good work in you will bring it to completion at the day of Jesus Christ."   Phil. 1:6

Country Style

September 25, 1969

A cheerful "Cock-a-doodle-doo" drifted across the neighbor's fields this morning, and I realized that I had been missing this familiar farm sound. I had not heard a rooster's greeting for some time. "Cock-a-doodle-doos" throughout the day used to be as much a part of farm atmosphere as the brake screeching and sirens represented the sounds of the city. A rooster's crowing is a good comfortable sound that seems to say, "Good morning! God's in His heaven; all's right with the world."

But all roosters are not the friendly "good morning" type. One year we boarded one that really belonged south of the border in cock-fighting country. When his squinty black eyes caught sight of you, you'd better run! He immediately headed in your direction, feathers ruffled, and you could almost see the anger radiating from him as he made a flying attack. Women and children were careful to look for his whereabouts before they went out the door. What a relief when his days came to an end!

Only a few farms house chickens any more. In past days chickens were a very essential part of farm living. The eggs bought the groceries; the rooster was the alarm clock; and when unexpected company came, the farmer's wife ran out to the chicken house (instead of the supermarket) grabbed a rooster and served fried chicken for supper. Before the days of freezers and refrigerators, chickens were necessary if the housewife was to have fresh meat and eggs on hand.

ARE YOU ready!

One of these nights Jack Frost will make his first visit and the wise have been collecting old sheets, blankets, and various nondescript articles to cover their flowers and tomatoes. These coverings will be protection from Jack Frost's deadly touch. Some of the coverings are not so pretty, but when they are removed at the light of day, underneath stand the lovely flowers and tomatoes, safe and beautiful.

IN TIMES of danger and temptation, God does the same for us!

"He shall cover thee with his feathers and under His wings shalt thou trust." Ps. 91:4

Country Style

October 2, 1969

The corn silage wagons are rolling. They are bringing the cornfield home to the silos in a chewed up, ready for serving form.

Silage is one of those meal-stretchers, which we can compare to our macaroni or rice. Bits of nourishing greens, mixed with meaty chunks of corn on the cob, make it a choice meal-in-one for the cattle and milk cows.

The farmer is glad to have plenty of food on hand, handy for feeding, for forecasters are already warning us of another rough winter. Even the little wooly bear caterpillar is forecasting a hard winter. This year they say that he is black from stem to stern, and blacker than ever before, which is supposed to indicate a rough winter.

Anyway, it's wise to be prepared, bad weather or not!

THREE LITTLE kittens are trying to get adjusted to country living. They just left a town home to spend the winter in our barn. Here they may have the advantage of plenty of nice warm milk, fresh from the cow, but I'm sure it is different living in a world of animals after living with people.

GET OUT your jackets and sweaters.

During the summer, we tried to stay out of the sun's rays, but now when the fall weather is upon us, we appreciate every bit of sunshine.

Today the little kittens are playing on the sunny side of the barn. Here they jump, run and tumble, and then they stretch out and let the sun's rays warm them. A picture of contentment. It doesn't seem to matter that fall is here when you stay on the sunny side.

LIFE HAS its sunny side too, where we can bask in the sunshine of His love...

"Make Thy face to shine upon thy servant; and teach me thy statutes." Ps. 119:135

Country Style

October 9, 1969

Football - where twenty-two big husky fellows spend a whole afternoon or evening fighting over one little pigskin!

I look out my window and watch our live pigskins that are still running around on their own legs. There are times when the farmer would like to give them a good kick too. For instance, when they burrow under the fence and break out.

About the time the pigskin season is over, the farmer's live ones will be heading for their last down too. The farmer hopes the final score will be a little in his favor.

THE COUNTRY kitchen is a busy, fragrant place these days. While the farmer's silage crew prepares food for the animals, the farmer's wife is busy preparing food for the crew.

About this time of the year we get hungry for doughnuts, pumpkin pie and homemade bread. Fall weather seems to increase appetites. And the aroma of coffee is especially tempting on a cool fall morning.

EACH YEAR when the corn husks get dry and their leaves start turning brown, the farmer makes a special trip into his cornfield to spy out the land - to see if the crop is rich or poor, and to determine if it is ready for harvest.

He walks up and down the rows, picking ears of corn at random, and then brings home a sample of the fruit of his land.

This year the farmer returned, displaying a bouquet of large golden ears, covered with hard, dented kernels, and announced that the time had come to get his cornpicker out.

This peek at the harvest filled him with enthusiasm to get into his fields and bring home his corn. What he has been working for all year is about to climax in piles of beautiful golden corn. A happy ending!

AFTER WE get a peek at God's promises, we are enthusiastic and anxious to claim them for our own...

"Behold, the Lord your God has set the land before you; go up, take possession, as the Lord, the God of your fathers, has told you; do not fear or be dismayed."   Deut. 1:21

Country Style

October 16, 1969

Decisions in the spring.
Decisions in the fall.
But "if" and "when" to buy some cattle.
Is the hardest decision of all!

Farming is no regular weekly paycheck kind of job, but an exciting (or dangerous) wait-and-see-how-we-come-out one. In the spring the farmer takes a risk as he places seed in the ground. But in the fall the farmer is taking an even greater risk as he places steers in his feedyards. To be a farmer you must have a touch of gambler in your soul.

Already many farmers have made their decisions and you can tell it by the noisy calves in their yards. They bawl both night and day.

At the fair this fall I saw a little boy crying and crying. No one could comfort him because he was lost. I suppose that's the way these calves feel in their new strange surroundings. And they noisily react in exactly the same way.

TODAY THE neighbor's grove is beautiful in shades of gold and rust and brown. The vine on the fence has turned deep red, and the sky is brightest blue. The breeze has a touch of chill to it, and some leaves are tumbling down. Perfect October weather.

OCTOBER IS a birthday month in our family.

Happiness...is birthdays and birthday wishes. Happiness is a surprise birthday cake from a friend. And happiness is the discovery that your family doesn't mind that you are a year older.

"Happiness is like perfume; you can't spray it on others without getting some on yourself." "Happiness doesn't depend upon what happens outside of you but on what happens inside of you. "Happiness doesn't come from doing what we like to do but from liking what we have to do."

And a picture of happiness... is a little granddaughter eyeing her two-candle birthday cake. "Happy birthday, Kristen!"

YOU CAN'T pursue happiness and catch it, but the Bible has some good happiness advice...

"O taste and see that the Lord is good! Happy is the man who takes refuge in him!" Ps. 34:8

Country Style

October 23, 1969

It was a GRAND OPENING.
The farmer removed the fence that had held them back, and the curious and the hungry streamed through to sample hay at the new hay feeder. They couldn't wait to try eating hay in new and different surroundings. All day long, out of every opening there protruded a chewing cow's head. The milk cows acted just as excited as people when there is a new eating place in town.

YOU CAN'T hold back the dawn, and neither can we hold on to a beautiful autumn. The first snowfall that came so unexpectedly taught us that. There stood the petunias and the dahlias bravely blooming in the snow. We hated so to give them up.

The flowers have been especially beautiful this fall, and we have been doing all we could to prolong their days. My mums have been so slow in blooming that I have been determined to keep them alive long enough so that they would have a chance to bloom. The covering still goes over them every evening.

But putting a covering over my bed of red petunias several weeks ago backfired on me. I ended up with more damage than from a frost. The protection was adequate, but I hadn't considered the dog. Pepper must have decided that the old blanket laying over the flowers would make a better bed than her old rug, because that is where she spent the night. The next morning when I removed the covering, only the plants on the outside of the patch still stood fresh and upright. The rest had a crushed and slept-in look. You can't win them all!

THE FLOWERS that have been smitten by Jack Frost look very sad, but we can't spend all winter grieving over them. Rather, we have something to look forward to - a hope...that when spring arrives many of these flowers will grow again, and bloom again, perhaps even more beautiful than they did this year.

HOPE is a magic and a mighty force that can carry us through disappointments and sorrows of all varieties and of all dimensions...
"Why are you cast down, O my soul, and why are you disquieted within me? Hope in God; for I shall again praise him, my help and my God." Ps. 43:5

Country Style

October 30, 1969

The birds are heading south.

These days our lawn is a rest stop where they take time to relax while they snatch a bite to eat before starting out again. Each evening the grove reverberates with boisterous twitterings as they gather for bird reunions and farewell parties.

The birds travel lightly and never grow too attached to their nests. How tragic it would be if they fussed and fixed and loved their home up north too dearly to give it up and move south. Then their dear little nest would eventually be the death of them.

THESE BUSY fall days are the time of most farm accidents. The farmer's wife has a vague uneasy feeling as each day the farmer wrestles with the corn picker or untangles the combine. If you could listen to her heart, you would probably hear these God-ward thoughts...

"Father, bless my husband today as he goes about his work.

Bless his hands, Lord, as he uses them to bring in the harvest. And earn our daily bread.

Keep them from clumsiness as he works with his machinery.

Keep them cautious when they must be in dangerous places.

Keep them steady as he controls tremendous horsepower.

All I can do is worry, Lord,

BUT Your hands are strong and capable of guidance and entirely trustworthy.

So I place him and his day with you.

Make my hands especially loving these busy days.

And thank you, God, for letting us again walk hand in hand through the exciting days of seedtime and harvest."

                        Amen

"I sought the Lord, and he answered me, and delivered me from all my fears."   Ps. 34:4

Country Style

November 6, 1969

Fall Beauty

Twin birch trees standing side by side.
Milk-white bark peeking through golden leaves.
Lovely birches delicately glistening in the autumn sun
Give me a Joyce Kilmer feeling.
And I stand in awe
at the artistry of God.

IT LOOKS like cotton-picking time. The burst milkweed pods with their white balls of fluff still clinging to the stem resemble cotton plants. But no farmer wants to harvest this soft silky stuff...for it is weed seeds.

"A BIRD in the hand is worth two in the bush" would be translated by the farmer today as "an ear of corn in the bin is worth a hundred ears of corn in the field." He has nightmares of a good snowfall that would interfere with his corn-picking.

The farmer is anxious enough to get his corn picked but much of it is too wet to crib. I guess he'll have to do what the housewife does when she wants to wash clothes on a rainy day - use the dryer!

THINGS I noticed the first day of Standard Time:
- The milk cows patiently waiting for the farmer, with a slightly puzzled look as if they were wondering why he was an hour late.
- Babies ready for their afternoon naps before they had their noon meal.
- The dog sitting by the back door waiting for her food an hour before suppertime.
- Feeling it was time for bed, but the clock telling us it was too early.

Babies and animals are at a disadvantage because they can't tell time. They just have to go by their built-in feelings.

LIFE CAN be frustrating. Changes here and changes there. We are always being asked to adjust to something or someone. How good it is to know there is One who is unchanging and dependable, day after day, year after year and age after age.

"For I am the Lord – I do not change."   Mal. 3:6

Country Style

November 13, 1969

ODDBALL

Do you know a farmer
Who planted all his seeds
In rows as straight as arrows
Without a sign of weeds?
His tractor starts like lightning
His cows give extra milk
His chickens all lay double yolks
The whole place runs like silk
Well, if you know this farmer
Then you better raise a fuss
'Cause he surely is an odd-ball
And not really one of us!
                M. E. Labor

SO WHAT if it rains on your soybeans, and the tractor starts missing during corn-picking? If you have been farming for any length of time, you know it's all in the farming game!

Each year we wait for a special kind of a day. We want it to be sunshiny, but it must be cool enough to get us in gear. - And then we do the storm window job!

The farmer's wife feels almost as relieved when this is finished as the farmer does when his corn is all picked. She's ready for winter!

EACH LINE of work has its own special shop talk. "Leeward" and "knots' have meaning to seafaring people. Wall-Streeters understand "bulls" and "bears", and so also you almost have to be talking to another farmer to carry on a farm conversation.

It doesn't take many minutes of visiting with a stranger before you discover if he has ever lived on a farm. If he asks intelligent questions and can converse for any length of time on farm subjects, you know he didn't spend all of his life in the city. Farm talk can be almost like speaking another language to someone who doesn't know about corn-heads and moisture tests.

Our speech reflects our line, whether we want it to or not.

"For as He which hath called you is holy, so be ye holy in all manner of conversation."
                I Peter 1:15

Country Style

November 20, 1969

Corn-picking - Old Style

They say "in those days" farmers hardly went to bed. Some just slipped their suspenders on a hook and hung out in the barn instead.

They were up at 4 a.m. to get the chores all done and harness up the horses before the rising sun.

Then off the farmer went with his hired man...for another day of picking corn "by hand".

The teams of horses rarely ever needed "Whoa". The right speed for picking corn they just seemed to know.

"Bang! Bang! on the bang-board was the only sound you'd hear. There were no trucks or tractors loudly changing gear.

At noon and night they'd head for home with their golden loads, all tired out and weary from all the corn they'd "throwed". And you had done a good day's work, everyone would say, if you picked 80 to 100 bushels in a day. Out there in the darkness they'd shovel off each ear. The corn-pickers got paid so much for every bushel there.

NOW - the mechanical picker rips off more corn in fifteen minutes than a man could do in one whole day. But the farmer has to pay for such speed and efficiency, for corn-pickers and combines cost all the way from five to twenty thousand dollars.

THEY'RE COMING out of the walls!

It's box-elder bug time and they're here. Most homes are fighting the battle of the bugs. When you think you have gotten rid of the last one, there comes another crazily zooming at you. I guess they have to have their day.

THE PIGS are delighting in a daily menu of ear corn. It makes them almost as excited as a good Norwegian when he discovers lefse on the table.

The new corn is soft and tasty, and the farmer doesn't even need to call them. When they see him head for the corn wagon, they come running. About this time, if pigs could express gratitude, they would probably "oink" out, "You're so good to me!"

WE HAVE Someone who takes care of us too, and each day we discover new treats he has in store...

"As for me, I am poor and needy; but the Lord takes thought for me." Ps. 40:17

Country Style

November 27, 1969

The Pilgrims really started something when they served turkey for the first Thanksgiving dinner. Now it just doesn't seem like Thanksgiving without it.

What if they had served pheasant or rabbit?

What do you do when Tom Turkey becomes the family pet? Turkeys don't have a lovable look and scare most people with their deep-throated "gobble - gobble - gobbles". It's hard to imagine a big turkey tagging you around...**because he is friendly!!**

But there have been families who have become so attached to one that they had roast beef for Thanksgiving. They just couldn't bear to think of taking bites from familiar turkey wings and legs.

The Secret

The curious cow remarked one
   day while chewing on a cud of
   hay...
"People are a funny brand - our
   farmer I can't understand.
His corn is wet, the mortgage's
   due, but I just never see him
   blue.
Even though some things go
   wrong, still he whistles out a
   song."

Then spoke up the wise old cat
"That man is smart; I'll tip my
   hat!
I get around...and I have found
that people either SMILE or
   FROWN.
Some tarnish life with discontent,
while other people's days are spent
in counting all the blessings sent.
Happiness is quite an art.
- The secret is a grateful heart."

THERE IS a Thanksgiving game that is guaranteed to be quite a revelation of the sometimes little and funny things that make our lives fuller and happier. Count your personal blessings, using the letters of the alphabet as a guide. Let your answers come brainstorming (whatever comes to mind) for example: "A" - jars of Applesauce in the basement, Anti-freeze on the car, Aunt Rachel's fruit salad recipe, etc. "B" - babies (maybe there's a special one), snow boots, books, etc., etc...

It's fun and it'll give you a thankful heart.

THE MORE you give thanks, the happier you are! Gratitude is a good feeling. But you get the greatest happiness when you say "Much obliged!" to God...

"What shall I render to the Lord for all his bounty to me?"
Ps. 116:12

Country Style

December 4, 1969

Already we are on the last page of the calendar. December is here.

The scenery has changed since last month. The trees that were lovely robed in golden leaves now stand bare in dark silhouette, revealing every twig and twiglet that the leaves had been hiding before.

There is a certain grace and plain beauty about a tree in winter. Now we can see all their attractive shapes and dainty twig work. Each tree has a different makeup. Some have a bough that is way out of proportions, or a gnarled look that makes us imagine that it had a hard life. We are impressed with the muscled sinewy look of some trees, and then there is the spindly fine-boned texture of the Chinese Elms.

But we never tire of studying the apple tree. Spring, summer and fall and winter the apple tree gives us something interesting to watch. Now we can detect every interesting curve of its branches. Some boughs hang low, perhaps from years of being too heavily laden with fruit. Several apples still hang way up at the top where no one could reach them. An old apple tree is a friendly piece of nature.

PILES OF bright golden corn brighten up the landscape. Some of it lays spread on the ground because the ears were too wet to crib. It's shining golden color attracts the eye like the sparkle of a diamond. Maybe there are golden sunbeams encased in those kernels. I have always wondered how green plants could produce such beautiful orange-colored ears.

STRIPS OF black plowing make designs in the countryside. Now most of the cornfields have a ransacked look for after corn-pickers and combines have been through them they are an empty, worthless mess of broken stalks and discarded husk. Here the cattle spend their days, lunching on the ears that were left behind.

SUNSETS come earlier every day as the days shorten into winter. And there have been some gorgeous ones. Some evenings all the little clouds in the sky are tinted pink as part of the grand finale of a December day.

AND WE get ready for the grand finale of the year - Christmas. There is much preparing to be done. Shopping, baking, and getting our homes and our hearts ready for the birthday of the King.

"Prepare the way of the Lord, make His paths straight."   Luke 3:4

Country Style

December 11, 1969

These days a little squirrel is busy scampering up and down the big corn pile that is located across the road from my kitchen window. This little fellow is having the time of his life. I suppose it is something like turning a child loose in the candy store - there is so much to pick from, he just doesn't know where to start.

As he climbs frantically around, he probably is in the same predicament as the farmer several weeks ago - he realizes there is plenty of corn to be had, if he can only get it stashed away before the snow comes.

AGAIN THIS year many grandpas and elderly uncles were seen aboard the tractors as they hauled corn, or were busy unloading wagons or watching the corncribs. These former farmers came out of retirement to lend a helping hand.

When you have spent most of your autumns bringing in the corn crop, you miss the excitement that goes with corn-picking, and you kind of enjoy having a part in it again. And besides, experienced helpers were very much needed.

AT CHRISTMAS time we expect and want only joy, happiness and love, but as we look around we become aware that this isn't always possible. There is the family who just experienced bereavement; the bedfast friend who is suffering and may not see much of the new year; the family who is separated at this special family time. It seems that sickness, death and heartache don't take a Christmas holiday.

Our hearts reach out in sympathy and it is hard for us to understand how Christmas can have any meaning for them.

- But that's what Christmas is all about!

"He hath appointed Me to preach the gospel to the poor;

He hath sent Me to heal the brokenhearted, to preach deliverance to the captives, and recovering of sight to the blind, to set at liberty them that are bruised."   Luke 4:18

God bless them everyone!

Country Style

December 18, 1969

One by one the farmers are parking their corn-pickers for another year. They breathe a sigh of relief and mutter "Finally!" and "It's about time!"

Now the farmer's wife can get out the Christmas decorations. The farmer couldn't stomach them before. They only seemed to remind him of how late in the season it was. It was like rubbing salt in a wound. Now that the corn-picking is over, they both can get at other things.

The toy departments are loaded with all kinds of new, clever and wonderful toys. With the titles of Grandpa and Grandma, we now have an excuse for browsing there again. The years fly by but dolls still hold a place of prominence, and shopping for a dolly is probably just as much fun for Grandma as receiving it will be for little Kristen.

MUSIC IS everywhere. We are enjoying both old and new Christmas songs and we find ourselves unconsciously singing them as we go about our daily chores.

THESE DAYS before Christmas can't be spent only baking beautiful cookies and Christmas goodies, there still must be meat and potato meals and the common tasks of washing, ironing and washing the milking machine are still a necessity. Even though it is the week before Christmas, the farmers are busy with such un-Christmasy things as caring for sows that are pigging, or cleaning the barn every day. The daily jobs and chores are still with us, but they become much more pleasant to the tune of "Hark the Herald Angels Sing" or "Silent Night".

AND IN our busy-ness, we wonder . . . "Oh, how shall I receive Thee?", and we discover we can do this all day long as we go about our work and our preparations for Christmas . . . .

"And whatever you do, in word or deed, do everything in the name of the Lord Jesus, giving thanks to God the Father through him." Col. 3:17

Country Style

December 25, 1969

The days pass so quickly in December that we sometimes wonder if we are being short-changed. Are there really twenty-four sixty-minute hours in each December day?

Before Christmas we need long days in order to get everything accomplished, and when Christmas is here and the family is together, we wish the days would never end. The only way we can lengthen them is by turning them into happy memories that can be relived, remembered and enjoyed at later times.

"HE'S JUST a old farmer!"
We've all heard this remark, and to some people farming is about as high on the totem pole of professions as sheep herding was nineteen hundred years ago. Tending sheep was a lowly occupation in those days. And yet, it is the shepherds that we sing about every Christmas – not the tentmakers or the shop-keepers or the fishermen. It is the shepherds that have a prominent place in the Christmas story.

Both shepherds and farmers are not beyond believing in miracles. Each year they see their seeds and animals multiply and the dead black earth turn to green feed for their animals.

Shepherds had to be brave. They kept watch on their sheep twenty-four hours a day, and they had no guns with which to shoot prowling animals. They had to rely upon their own strength, their rod and staff, and perhaps a faithful dog.

The shepherds were humble people, and had no grand illusions about their occupation. But we shouldn't sell the shepherds short.

SUPPOSE . . . .
While caring for your pigs one night an angel host appeared,
   would you be scared?
IF . . . . .
They announced a Savior's birth and invited you to see,
   would you go immediately?
WHEN . . . .
You had gazed upon the baby's face and your heart was all aglow,
   would you let your whole world know?
The Shepherds did.

May your Christmas end as happily as the shepherds' Christmas.
   "And the shepherds returned, glorifying and praising God for all they had heard and seen, as it had been told them."   Luke 2:20

Country Style

January 1, 1970

Happy New Year!

Each new year is a surprise package, and we handle it carefully because we don't know what it will hold, but we must be content to examine it one day at the time.

But it was a good Christmas!

The Christmas programs with darling little boys and girls, all dressed up in their new Christmas outfits, speaking their Christmas pieces, and older boys and girls using their talents to tell the Christmas story.

The days of Christmas were especially happy because a little two-year-old brightened up our home, and we again were privileged to see the excitement of Christmas through a two-year-old's eyes.

Christmas cards from far and near brought news of friends and relatives that we hadn't heard from for a year.

Lefse, krumkakke, berlinerkrandser and traditional Christmas goodies were enjoyed again.

Even the scenery was right for a South Dakota Christmas. Snow covered the dirty and messy fields and dressed up our world in spotless white.

As the snow fell, even the animals out in the fields took on a "flocked" look that gave the same effect as the flocked Christmas trees.

The packages have all been opened and we are rejoicing because of the love behind each gift. Now it is time to write the thank-you notes that try to express the feelings that are in our hearts. We say "It is just what I needed!", "Beautiful", "It grows more precious with each day!"

AND WE try to write a thank-you note for the original Christmas gift, and we use all of these same phrases, but are left speechless because the feelings in our hearts can't be expressed in words...

"Thanks be to God for His inexpressible gift." 2 Cor. 9:15

Country Style

January 8, 1970

GOD'S SPECTACULAR

All night He worked, and as the
  sun came up
We gasped to see the beauty of it
  all.
Each tree, each twig
Was individually wrapped in white.
The sky was just the softest blue.
Long shadows stretched upon the
  dazzling snow
And little diamonds twinkled
  everywhere.
We "ooh!" and "aah!" to see the
  snow we so much dread
Become a quiet winter wonderland
  instead.

1970 - the beginning of a new decade.

As we take a backward look at the 60's with their thirty-inch rows, 150 bushel an acre corn yields, and the many empty farm homes resulting from bigger and bigger farming operations, we wonder what the next ten years will hold.

Will farmers be using computers to tell them when to sell their hogs and cattle, and sit at a switchboard and run their tractors by remote control? Or perhaps, as the population increases, they will be selling more of their grain for cornflakes and oatmeal, instead of feeding it all to their livestock!

One thing we know, farming will keep changing.

"**A LITTLE** child shall lead them."

We are so stingy with our love and our expressions of it. Having two-year-old Kristen spend a few days with us made me aware of how wonderful it feels and how much brighter the day becomes when someone sprinkles your day with "I love you's!"

We never knew when it was coming, but all of a sudden a serious little voice would say "Know what?", and as we answered "No, What?" she would affectionately state "I wuv you!" This showing of affection was as much a part of her day as eating and napping.

How much happier our world would be if we all followed her example!

"Know what?"
"I wuv you!"
"Make love our aim."
                I Cor. 14:1

Country Style

January 15, 1970

The big brown envelope has arrived.

Farmers all across the United States are busy filling out their agricultural census blanks. But it isn't as simple as listing - "Mr., Mrs., the kids and the dog." A lot more details are required. The farmer must take inventory of everything and report it in tons, bushels and litters.

We are reminded of how varied agriculture is by the many crops suggested - nut trees, cotton, citrus fruits, grapevines, lettuce and melons. Every farmer in these United Stated doesn't just raise corn, oats and soybeans.

Taking census isn't something new. It has been done through the ages. We will have to admit that it is easier for us to sit in the warm house and have our census taken by mail than having to make a hundred mile trip like Mary did almost two thousand years ago.

A PILE of fuzz is telltale evidence of a hunting expedition. Our area may be closed to jack rabbit hunting, but how do you inform the dogs? Chasing rabbits comes as naturally to dogs as eating or sleeping, and to them rabbits are always in open season.

SEVERAL DOGS have shown up lately that make us shiver in our boots. They aren't four-legged ones either, but the "sun dogs" that accompany and forecast cold weather. We are never happy to see them. But they are more accurate in their forecasting than weathermen.

I READ an interesting editorial suggesting that milk advertising should be more sexy and hep. In this day and age, it said, no one wants to be told to buy something because it's good for you. You must tell people it will make them more attractive, slimmer, it's the "in" thing, an exciting drink, or that it will provide status and a sense of belonging. These are the sales pitches that "turn on" today's buyer.

But satisfied customers are still the best advertisement. A baby crying for a bottle is trying in his own way to tell us "I'd rather fight than switch!" And asking for a second helping is an advertisement in itself.

And...
"If you have tasted the Lord's goodness and kindness, cry for more, as a baby cries for milk. Eat God's Word - and grow strong in the Lord."
I Peter 2:2,3 (Living Letters)

Country Style

January 22, 1970

Thirteen below!

Will the car start? Are the water fountains frozen up?

And the mention of the wind chill temperature is enough to make us shiver while sitting before the fire.

I've noticed that on cold days we go around comparing thermometers. In a way we sort of brag about the weather. Maybe it makes us feel more rugged and tough. If someone asks how cold it was at our place, there usually is a tone of pride in our voice if we can report a temperature a degree or two colder than theirs.

THESE DAYS the milk cows walk with a slow careful gait that makes us wonder if they have rheumatism. I suppose the reason for the slow going is the patches of ice and frozen ruts in the yards. Cows aren't so dumb! They don't want to risk a tumble any more than people do.

But the calves don't worry about such things any more than children do. Winter is for fun and off they go - running, jumping and sliding.

PEOPLE ALWAYS seem to have a softer heart in the winter. We can't turn away either man or beast on a cold winter day.

One day I was surprised to see a little pointed face peering at me through the pane in the door, its little black nose pressed against the glass. There stood a little dog on its hind legs, looking for something. Love? food? or shelter?

I don't know where it came from, but by its looks and actions, it has been trying to worm its way into our affections and become one of our farm family.

Pepper reacts to this new addition in the same way that a little child often does when a new baby brother or sister arrives and he or she no longer receives all the attention.

You almost have to be a referee to feed the dogs. As long as you stand there, Pepper will only consume her portion, but when you leave she bounds over to finish off the new dog's share too. She has no compassion for a hungry starving fellow-dog.

It's fun to see how people are kinder to people in the winter. They are always willing to help someone who is stalled, and are quick to get out and give someone a push. I don't think anyone would turn away someone from their door on a cold snowy night.

HELPING PEOPLE in need can be exciting when you remember Hebrews 13:1,2... "Continue to love each other with true brotherly love. Don't forget to be kind to strangers, for some who have done this have entertained angels without realizing it" (Living Letters)

Country Style

January 29, 1970

LAND OF VARIETY

In spring our world's a garden,
   as pretty as you please;
In summer, a busy factory,
   where farmer with nature meets:
In fall, it is a warehouse,
   containing our increase,
But when we reach the winter,
   our world's a big deep freeze!

On a cold morning, it takes a lot of willpower to leave the nice warm spot in the bed and get up to face the chilly world.

The pigs seem to have this problem too, because these days they don't show up for breakfast until it is almost noon. There is no activity at the self-feeders or water fountain on a cold morning. They put off the getting up process as long as they can.

TWENTY-FIVE or fifty years ago, the women would have taken advantage of these cold days by setting up the quilt frame and getting busy with a quilt.

In those days, in order to keep the family warm on cold nights, the beds were loaded down with quilts made of gay prints or crazy-quilt designs, filled with wool batting and tied with bright tufts of yarn. Ever so often the ladies had to take time out to replenish their supply.

The coming of electric blankets and warmer houses has kind of made old-fashioned quilts disappear from the scene.

"**SLOW AS** molasses in January!"

January's cold may slow down the milk cows, the pigs, and some motors, but the winter hasn't taken the pep out of everything.

Today we saw a beautiful horse racing across a snowy pasture - and seeming to enjoy it! (Or else it was trying to keep warm.) It made an attractive scene as the snow flew in all directions each time its feet touched the ground.

Horses were born to run, and I'm sure they find enjoyment doing what they were designed for.

WE WILL find happiness too...when we do the things we were created for...

"For we are His workmanship, created in Christ Jesus for good works, which God prepared beforehand that we should walk in them."   Eph. 2:10

Country Style

February 5, 1970

"Ghosts of Biafra."

These days it's hard to sit up to the table without thoughts of starving Biafran children. As we dish up the mashed potatoes, roast beef and gravy, we wish they were within reach so we could fill up plates for some of them too.

The conscience of a farmer would never let an animal on his farm starve. Allowing anything to go without food goes against his grain. When the farmer sees a need, he is quick to do something about it. From his pail of milk, the kittens and dogs get all they want to drink. If a lamb has lost its mother, he personally bottle-feeds it, and sometimes he even uses an eye dropper to get food into a baby pig.

But this Biafran situation is so frustrating because we see the tragedy, and are left helpless to do anything about it - only to let the knowledge and photos haunt us. May it soon be straightened out.

READY. GET SET. GO!

Today people expect their equipment to be in a state of readiness. They haven't time to wait for "Ready" and "Get set". It's got to be "Go" right now.

They haven't time to waste waiting for a radio or TV to warm up, or heating water for a bath. Today their cars and tractors are plugged into electric heaters so they are always ready to go.

When the Model T was "King of the Road", getting a car started was a major operation. You expected to spend some time on it. You approached the task with a teakettle of hot water in your hand to hurry the process, and you knew the car wouldn't start the first time you turned the crank. Patiently it was cranked and cranked and cranked again.

In the wintertime the radiator was kept carefully covered with old coats, robes and quilts. After trying everything else, you could always harness up the horses and give it a pull, which is more than can be done to today's cars.

Our "I want what I want WHEN I want it" attitude has brought about all kinds of pushbutton inventions. If people were in such a state of readiness as their equipment, how much would and could be accomplished.

GOD delights in readiness too.

"My heart is ready, O God, my heart is ready!

I will sing, I will sing praises! Awake, my soul!" Ps. 108:1

Country Style

February 12, 1970

VALENTINE PRAYER

Give us a denim love
    that's tough enough to stand the strain
    of every days and still remain;
    strong enough to take financial stress
    and warm enough to melt our selfishness.
    A love that's comfortable and brings
    enjoyment in the little things.
    True, genuine and honest to the core,
    A denim love that's guaranteed to wear
    and each year grow better than before.
                    AMEN.

LOVE IS "give and take". It's more than words. If it's there, it will come through in actions that will bring pleasure and happiness to the loved one.

She bakes a chocolate cake, even though she's on a diet, because he likes it. That's love!

He gives up buying a tractor cab so she can have the carpeting she's been wanting. That's love!

She spends the afternoon at the fair letting him show her the new machinery. That's love!

Usually men live in two worlds - the business work-a-day world and their home life. Not the farmer. His home life and his work life are all interwoven into one piece. His wife is in on all of his business life. She is there to rejoice when the cow has twins and pat him on the back when the corn goes a hundred bushels to the acre. She is there with a hand to hold when hail comes or the pigs get sick. The farmer's wife cannot separate her home life from the farm life. She must always be there to help, to cheer, to encourage, to love and understand.

YOU MAY think it's just an old seed catalog, but let me tell you what it can do.

Seed catalogs stir us up to new dreams and give us ideas for summer beauty and a longing for fresh garden eating.

You have to have a dream before you have a goal, and you have to have a goal before you get into action. Poring over a seed catalog starts the ball rolling and soon results in ordering seeds, plants and bulbs, which in turn forces you to roll up your sleeves to care for them.

Next summer when these flowers are blooming and the pods of peas are hanging on the vine, remember that it all started the day a little old seed catalog came in the mail.

IT MAY take a seed catalog to stir us up to make our world more beautiful, but WE must stir up our world...

"And let us consider how to stir up one another to love and good works."   Heb. 10:24.

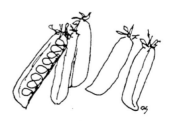

Country Style

February 19, 1970

The sun shines bright on our old winter world. Today is a lovely day. The temperature is high enough to bring on a slight thaw towards noon, but not warm enough to destroy the snow. Through my window I see a group of sparrows lunching on the few apples that were left at the top of the apple tree. These apples have defrosted enough so that the birds can make a meal of them. It's like digging into the freezer for dessert.

From another window I see the cows lounging on new bedding, and they look as contented lying out there as if they were sunning themselves on some sunny southern beach.

On these kind of days, the farmer's wife feels like getting out too, and you may see her head off for a day of shopping or an afternoon of club, ladies' aid or visiting.

When winter treats us so nicely, we won't complain but enjoy each fine day that comes along.

CAN SHE bake a cherry pie?

I'm sure housewives all over America have served cherries in one way or another during the month of February.

The legend of George Washington and the cherry tree initiated the tradition of serving cherry pie and other cherry desserts during the month of his birth. Bright red cherry desserts give a sparkling color to drab winter menus.

A housewife not only uses her baking ability to celebrate certain occasions, but she also gets to mixing ingredients when she wants to sympathize or soothe a loved one.

When her teen-age daughter has a broken heart, a woman sets to baking a cherry tart. When her son's team loses, when his dog is dead, she bakes a chocolate cake or homemade bread. When the crops are a disappointment and the bills are high, she bakes her family an apple pie. It is her way of showing she understands and cares. At times like these, her family cannot only feel her love, but they can literally taste it.

WHEN WE see to what extent a mother goes to give comfort and love, these words which our Heavenly Father whispers hold more meaning for us...

"As one whom his mother comforts, so I will comfort you."

Isa. 66:13

Country Style

February 26, 1970

"What am I bid?"

Attending farm auctions is the farmer's pastime during the winter. That auction bill hanging on a wall or printed in the newspaper is a special invitation for him to come and see if he can find a bargain. And whether he buys anything or not, the afternoon gets to be a get-together with other farmers as they meet and visit, and gather at the stand for a cup of hot coffee.

But the undertones of the day are sad. Usually the reason for the sale is an unhappy one - either death has touched the family, or setbacks and bad luck or illness has made the farm family have to call it quits.

Out on the ground set their possessions for neighbors and strangers to examine and handle. The things that they looked at with love and pride now in the glare of the bright sunlight show all their signs of wear, and in other people's eyes often have little dollar and cents value.

It's hard to see the bidders look at their things with such critical eyes. The owner gets a lump in his throat as he watches people bid on the cows that he knows well enough to call by name.

And his tractor. He remembers the day it was shining and new. It still has lots of life left in it, but today no one seems excited about it. They say it is too small for today's farming needs. Some farmer will probably buy it as a second tractor.

But the things he calls junk are getting all the attention - old cream cans, an old wagon wheel, an old trunk, and anything that goes under the category of antiques.

All afternoon the auctioneer's voice runs on and on. "I've got five, who'll give me six?", repeated at such a rapid rate that he can hardly be understood. The crowd of people follow him around from one area to another, trudging through snow and mud.

And then it comes to an end. They look around as the possessions that were so recently theirs, are loaded up. They are thankful if the weather cooperated and a crowd gathered, but most especially if their possessions sold for what they were worth.

"Going. Going. Gone!"

The items up for auction may represent many years of farming, but there is one thing that did not go up for auction. It is the memories of the years they spent on the farm, of the dreams that did come true, of a little family growing up here, of the years of working, loving and living. These are treasures that can never be taken away from them. But now life must move on.

BEHOLD, what I have seen to be good and to be fitting is to eat and drink and find enjoyment in all the toil with which one toils under the sun the few days of his life which God has given him, for this is his lot."
Ecc. 5:18